AIMING FOR AN A IN A-LEVEL POLITICS

Sarra Jenkins

HODDER
EDUCATION
AN HACHETTE UK COMPANY

Acknowledgements

pp. 31-32 © The Economist Group Limited, London (April 2018)

With thanks to the CDARE team at the Sheffield Institute of Education for their assistance developing and reviewing this title.

Every effort has been made to trace all copyright holders, but if any have been inadvertently overlooked, the Publishers will be pleased to make the necessary arrangements at the first opportunity.

Although every effort has been made to ensure that website addresses are correct at time of going to press, Hodder Education cannot be held responsible for the content of any website mentioned in this book. It is sometimes possible to find a relocated web page by typing in the address of the home page for a website in the URL window of your browser.

Hachette UK's policy is to use papers that are natural, renewable and recyclable products and made from wood grown in sustainable forests. The logging and manufacturing processes are expected to conform to the environmental regulations of the country of origin.

Orders: please contact Bookpoint Ltd, 130 Park Drive, Milton Park, Abingdon, Oxon OX14 4SE. Telephone: (44) 01235 827827. Fax: (44) 01235 400401. Email education@bookpoint.co.uk Lines are open from 9 a.m. to 5 p.m., Monday to Saturday, with a 24-hour message answering service. You can also order through our website: www.hoddereducation.co.uk

ISBN: 978 1 5104 2422 7

Typeset in Integra Software Services Pvt. Ltd., Pondicherry, India

Printed in India

A catalogue record for this title is available from the British Library.

Contents

Getting the most from this book

Aiming for an A is designed to help you master the skills you need to achieve the highest grades. The following features will help you get the most from this book.

Learning objectives

> A summary of the skills that will be covered in the chapter.

Exam tip

Practical advice about how to apply your skills to the exam.

Activity

An opportunity to test your skills with practical activities.

! Common pitfall

Problem areas where candidates often miss out on marks.

The difference between...

Key concepts differentiated and explained.

Annotated example

Exemplar answers with commentary showing how to achieve top grades.

Take it further

Suggestions for further reading or activities that will stretch your thinking.

The bottom line

> A summary of key points to take away from the chapter.

About this book

The study of politics is an exciting and constantly evolving discipline. Students undertake studies in politics for a range of reasons — from having a huge personal interest in local, national or global politics, to simply thinking it sounds interesting. Your starting base of knowledge is not, however, what will ultimately help you gain an A. Rather, your approach towards study, your study skills, and your determination to continually improve upon your work will be the key to your success. That's where this book comes in.

The focus of this book is to identify the skills necessary to achieve highly in politics, and show you how to develop them further. You will find sections in this book that demonstrate reading and note-taking skills as well as the different types of writing that you will need to employ in your final examination. These skills need to be developed over the whole two years (or one year, if you are doing AS) of your study; this is a companion to help you throughout all of your political studies, not a revision guide only to be opened at the end.

Your approach

Much has been written, and argued, recently about the 'growth mindset'. For students, this can all seem a bit lofty and theoretical. However, it boils down to a fairly simple principle:

How you **approach** your work will determine your success.

If, when you get an essay back from your teacher, you look only at the mark and then file it away, never again to see the light of day, you have not really engaged with the learning process. The same is true if, when you get a mark that disappoints you, you simply 'give up'. Instead, if you can remember that every essay you hand in to a teacher is merely practice for the final examination, you will find their comments and feedback are there not to discourage you, but to give you direction. It should help you to understand where your focus should be for improvement in your next practice and give you a hand in reflecting on not just your weaknesses, but also your strengths.

This book should help and support you in this process. From the very beginning of your A-level studies, if you can be well organised, know the exam board requirements, have a positive and engaged attitude towards learning, and use this book to help you improve your subject-specific skills, you should find that your marks improve and, hopefully, you will enjoy both the subject and learning more. In my experience, students who love their subjects show more convincing passion and well-argued persuasion throughout their writing.

It is worth noting that without such an attitude, you will not get the most out of this book. What many students want are shortcuts to success — you will not find them here as there are none, in this or in any other subject. There is plenty of advice that can be offered, but how you apply it is what will ultimately lead to your success.

The ten commandments

Before getting into the specifics of each skill, there is some generic advice that should underpin the whole of your A-level study:

1 **There is not one 'right' answer.** This is a common misconception and one you should put aside early on. The way in which you interpret both evidence and the questions make it possible to have two quite different, but highly scoring, answers.

2 **Equally, there is no 'right' formula to essay writing.** You will develop your own style as you apply advice, and that is exactly what you should be aiming for. The best essays have the passionate argument of the student who wrote it, not a generic description of everything they have learnt.

3 **A-level is a step up from GCSE.** Far more emphasis is placed on transferable skills such as analysis, evaluation and interpretation, rather than merely knowing 'stuff'. It is important to recognise that simply knowing examples is not the key to success.

4 **Know the requirements.** Know what your exam board wants, know the level descriptors, and certainly spend some time reading the question. If you know exactly what your target is, you are far more likely to hit it.

5 **Feedback on your work is the single most useful advice you will receive.** Feedback will give you advice that is specific to you and your writing. Use this, alongside this book, to know what your next target should be.

6 **Remember that this is a two-year course.** You are unlikely to be brilliant in your first essay, and there may be times when something flummoxes you. Do not allow this to put you off; your goal is the final exam.

7 **Read.** Reading is one of the biggest things that will help improve your writing. You might be reading textbooks, newspapers, academic journals or blogs. This is not only because you will learn more information, but because you will be exposed to different types of writing and this will help develop your own prose.

8 **Use every tool available to you.** Rely on more than just your lessons. Using this book is a good start, but also use your friends and their work, use your teacher, use your library, use the exam board documents on their websites, and use reliable sources on the internet.

9 **Be wary of the internet.** Know how to identify a reputable source (advice on which you can find later in this book) and be especially wary of essay-help/writing websites. If there is not one 'right' answer, it logically follows that these kinds of sites will be of limited use, and probably will undermine your confidence.

10 **Reflect.** You will only really improve your work if your continually reflect on the work you have already done and try to learn from your mistakes.

That said, the absolute best advice that can be offered is to enjoy your subject. Almost everything else will follow if you simply enjoy doing the work that is required to achieve highly. Politics is dynamic and in the news every day. It affects every aspect of everyone's lives. Understanding it can be both exhilarating and frustrating (especially at election time). The more enjoyment you find in politics, the more you discuss it with your friends and family, and the more you recognise that the work involved is your chance to engage with it, the more quickly you will see your grades improve.

Using this book

Each chapter in this book looks at developing a different skill. You will not be able to read it all at once and 'be good' at politics. Instead, you should aim to delve in and out of chapters as you are learning skills in your class and as you practise them in your own work.

- **Chapter 1** will give you a good outline of what you are going to study — this includes the skills your examiners look for and how you will be assessed. It will help you to understand the 'bigger picture' of the politics A-level.

- **Chapter 2** will teach you how to read effectively and quickly, and give you advice on what to read to help develop relevant political knowledge. You will also learn how to make notes that are useful and valuable, both in your lessons and from your reading.

- **Chapter 3** tackles the process of writing short, factual answers, including those that involve analysing sources. You'll gain advice on how to write these quickly and effectively to maximise your marks in the shortest time.

- **Chapter 4** addresses the wide range of skills involved in writing essays, from simply understanding the question to writing analytical and evaluative paragraphs, rather than merely being descriptive. It also illustrates the infrastructure that supports these essays — planning and structuring them, and reflecting on how to improve your own work.

- **Chapter 5** is for use as your exams approach. It reviews different ways in which you can revise, what to do in the exam hall...and what to do afterwards.

- **Appendix 1** is a reference for you to understand exactly what is in your exam and how you will be assessed. You can pop in and out of this reference section anytime you are trying to understand how your work fits into your overall exam structure.

- **Appendix 2** is space for you to reflect upon written work as you complete it as part of your course, to help you identify targets and develop your written ability.

In short, aim to use this book **alongside** your lessons and homework. Use the relevant chapters as you are set work to complete and always keep coming back to it when you review your work.

1 Your politics exam

The purpose of the exam

Many students dread the prospect of examinations. They loom in the background throughout your study and can be a cause of anxiety, with students thinking these 'tests' are designed to try and trip them up. Understanding that this is not the case is really useful. Rather, exams are an opportunity for you to demonstrate your academic skills and are, in fact, the reason that you have been studying. Having spent two years studying politics and developing your skills, you should relish the chance to show off what you have achieved. In truth, the better prepared you are, the more revision you have done, and the more opportunities for practice and improvement you have used, the less scary they become. For your teachers, universities and employers, the exams are a way of understanding what you have achieved over your time studying.

At A-level, the politics exam will assess a number of skills that you should have developed. Short-answer questions (such as Edexcel's 12-mark questions in Paper 3, and AQA's 9-mark questions in Papers 1, 2 and 3) look mostly at what you know. These questions mostly rely on core skills that you should have a good understanding of from your previous study. These are skills such as your ability to remember what you have been taught and use it to answer a question, selecting the most relevant and appropriate information.

In source questions (such as AQA's 25-mark question in Papers 1, 2 and 3, and Edexcel's 30-mark question in Papers 1 and 2), the exam is exploring your ability to comprehend information quickly, and identify the relevant arguments. Within this, you should be able to identify trends from data (such as statistics) and find comparable and contrasting arguments. You should also be able to supplement what you have identified from sources with your own knowledge, and use your advanced skills to argue about the value of the source, and the validity of the arguments that it suggests.

Finally, the essay questions (such as Edexcel's 24- and 30-mark questions in Papers 1, 2 and 3, and AQA's 25-mark questions in Papers 1, 2 and 3) are focused more on your advanced skills. You will most likely have to explore two sides of an argument, but if

> **! Common pitfall**
>
> From the outset, make sure you are aware that timing is everything. Know how long each type of question should take you and stick to it.

you simply focus on describing these arguments, you will not score highly. The exam is looking for you to show how each argument can be analysed, and for you to show reasoned judgement throughout, before reading an overall conclusion.

Take it further

Your exam board has a specification, past exam papers and lots of other documents on its website. Become familiar with these documents as ultimately they are what you are being judged against.

The difference between...

Core skills	Advanced skills
These are skills which require less thought either to carry out or to achieve. In theory, they are skills like 'remembering' and 'understanding'. In politics, the most common core skill you will use is the recall of factual information that you have been taught to describe how processes work, and similarities and differences for the short-answer questions.	These are skills that require far more critical thought from you, being more analytical about the information you have and evaluating its usefulness and significance. In politics, you will be especially using 'analysis' and 'evaluation' in the longer-answer questions where your work will be more argumentative and persuasive, involving a rationally formed judgement.

The examiner

You will probably hear your teacher talk about 'your examiner'. This is the person who marks your paper. While you do not need to know much about them, it is helpful to understand that your examiner is probably a teacher too — they are not looking to 'trip you up'. Nevertheless, you can try your best to make marking easier for them. This means nothing more than:

→ leaving a line between every paragraph

→ writing legibly — this does not mean being really neat. It just means making sure your work can be read.

→ answering the questions in the right place in your exam booklet

→ using only commonly understood political abbreviations

Assessment objectives and levels

Understanding the way that you are going to be assessed should help you to know more clearly the target you are aiming for. Assessment objectives (AOs) are just that — they are the target (objective) against which you will be judged (assessed). All exam boards have the same AOs, although they do not all give them the same weight. (See Appendix 1 for more information specifically on your exam board.)

Assessment objective 1 (AO1)

'Demonstrate knowledge and understanding of political institutions, processes, concepts, theories and issues.'

This AO is about **what you know**. This could involve political theory, such as demonstrating that you understand what political sovereignty is, or an example, such as knowing that Theresa May became the prime minister in 2016 when David Cameron resigned following the referendum on the UK's membership of the EU.

> ## ! Common pitfall
>
> Pick your pen wisely. Make sure it is one you have practised with previously — it really makes a difference. Also make sure the ink will not bleed through the pages — most exams are scanned in and this makes them very hard to read.

It is important to be aware that there is a difference between knowing something and understanding it. AO1 rewards both 'knowledge' and 'understanding', therefore simply regurgitating the notes you have taken in a lesson will not score very highly.

The difference between...

Knowing	Understanding
Knowing something means that you are able to recognise and probably describe something. In simple terms, this is being able to give definitions or describe political events.	If you understand something, you will be able to use what you know in different circumstances. In simple terms, you will be able to use your own words (rather than, say, those of a source) and apply your understanding to different examples, time periods or events.
For example: parliamentary sovereignty means that parliament is the source of all power in the UK.	For example: Parliament in the UK is 'sovereign', meaning it is the source of all power, so the Scottish Parliament and the Welsh Assembly exist only because Parliament says they can.

Assessment objective 2 (AO2)

'Analyse aspects of politics and political information, including in relation to parallels, connections, similarities and differences.'

This AO is all about the advanced skill of analysis. It is important when trying to understand AOs that you recognise each skill might be different for each subject. Therefore 'analysis' in this case means something specific to politics.

At a basic level, to analyse something means to take it apart and look in detail at what it is and how it works. This makes sense if you are talking about a clock, but students often find it more difficult to understand when talking about concepts. Therefore, for politics, we can say that analysis really means two things:

→ For any point that you have made, **what** is it and **why** does it work that way?

→ Can you make any **connections** from your point to something else — something in your own knowledge or something in the question you have been asked?

> **! Common pitfall**
>
> Your previous studies have probably relied upon 'knowing stuff'. Students are often too willing to spend lots of time describing information, yet this is worth well under half of the marks available.

> **! Common pitfall**
>
> It is important to remember that when you begin using judgement terms, you are moving from analysis to evaluation.

Annotated example 1.1

If you were faced with the question, 'To what extent can the Conservative Party be regarded as Thatcherite?', you might want to write a paragraph about the tax pledges of the Conservative Party in the 2017 election. However, this is only knowledge (AO1) — you know that they promised to raise the tax-free allowance for income tax and to raise the threshold for the highest tax rate of 40p to £50,000. For AO2 you would need to consider:

● What is a tax-free allowance, how does it work and what would the impact be?

● What is the higher tax rate, how does it work and what would the impact be?

● You could make connections to your own knowledge by comparing this to Conservative tax pledges in other elections, comparing the higher threshold to the average UK income, or comparing the outcome of these two pledges. You could make connections with the question by explaining how either of these could be considered Thatcherite, and considering which one could be considered more Thatcherite.

It is important that you break down the 'point' of your paragraph so you can use the resulting bits of information to make connections with your question. As you develop this skill, you will discover your paragraphs cannot be written to a formula — it is not possible to write an 'essay-by-numbers'. Instead, if you develop good analysis, you will find that each point you make raises more questions, which you can compare and make connections to.

Assessment objective 3 (AO3)

'Evaluate aspects of politics and political information, including to construct arguments, make substantiated judgements and draw conclusions.'

This AO rewards a different advanced skill: the skill of evaluation. Too often this is confused with simply drawing a conclusion at the end of an essay. Evaluation is something that should take place throughout your essay, as you judge the importance, strength and relevance of each point you have made. Where analysis is about breaking a point down, evaluation puts it back together and asks you to decide how valid an argument is. As part of this AO, you will receive marks for the quality of your own written argument. If you have simply described lots of points and the essay seems to be a set of vaguely related paragraphs, you will not score very highly. Rather, if you have set out your line of argument from the beginning, and then argued your point using evidence and showing why counter-arguments could be discounted, you are displaying far greater judgement in your work.

This judgement may be made in a number of ways, but the crucial thing is to explain your reasoning. Writing, 'Therefore, first-past-the-post should be reformed' is not evaluation. Instead, you have to show informed judgement based on what you have written and explain how you reached the opinion that this point is strong or weak. Students are usually good at explaining weakness, but you need to ensure you practise explaining why an argument is strong too.

 Exam tip

A key analytical theme to understand is that the answer to almost every question is 'it depends' — the key factor that each question hinges on is the context or circumstances. In analysing whether the US Supreme Court is too powerful, a basic answer is to look at what power it does, and does not have. A more nuanced answer is to know that its power is not set, it changes over time. Therefore, in what context or circumstances does its power increase or decrease, and does this affect your answer? This skill encompasses both AO2 and AO3. Despite this, you must always reach a clear, justified conclusion.

! Common pitfall

Students often think that 'more is better' — more arguments mean more marks. This is incorrect. Fewer arguments, well analysed and evaluated, are the key to high marks. You should not be worried about the points you have left out — presumably, you used judgement and decided they were of less importance.

The difference between...

Analysis (AO2)	Evaluation (AO3)
Analysis involves breaking down one process or event and looking at its specific details, explaining why it occurs and why it is important. Analysis should refer to the distinct and specific piece of AO1 — theories, examples, fact and figures — that precedes it. It is the equivalent of looking at how each of the cogs within a watch mechanism interacts with the others to cause the hands to move.	Evaluation means demonstrating how relevant the concept or process as a whole is to your question, and what judgement you can make of this argument. This is the equivalent of looking at the watch itself and asking why such a thing exists, and whether its existence is positive, negative, or perhaps both.

Activity

For each of the three assessment objectives, write a definition in your own words. This will help you make sense of all the examiner jargon and ensure you have understood the discussion above.

 Exam tip

The AOs are your target, not your structure. Students who try and work systematically through AO1, then AO2, then AO3 in each paragraph end up with clinical, uninspiring essays.

Synopticity

At various points in your exam, some of your marks are awarded for 'synopticity'. This means that instead of simply focusing on one individual topic and answering the question in isolation, you will be expected to draw on knowledge from the other topic areas that you have studied and explain contrasting interpretations. Most students will do this almost by accident — it is difficult to argue that first-past-the-post needs replacing without talking about democracy, yet these are two different topics in your specification.

Just being aware of this is usually enough, and it is not something that you should spend lots of time thinking about.

Assessment levels

When an examiner marks your work, the first thing they will do is try to place it in a 'level'. Each type of question has different levels. For example, the short-answer questions have three (AQA) or four (Edexcel) levels, and the longer-answer questions have five levels. Each level will have a description attached to it. Lower levels tend to include words like 'limited' and 'descriptive', and higher levels will include words like 'accurate' and 'balanced'. Once they have placed your essay in a level, they will then decide what mark it is worth within that level. Knowing these descriptors will help you understand what you are aiming to achieve, and they can all be found on your exam board's website.

Getting organised for study

Earlier, the importance of your approach to study was outlined. Before you even go to your first lesson, or open your first textbook, you need to ensure you have some idea of how to be organised for A-level study. This involves more than just having some paper and a pencil case in your bag.

To begin with, the most helpful way to organise your notes for A-level will be in a ring-binder or lever arch file. This will prove most helpful when you come to writing essays and you can pick out only the relevant notes you have made and reorganise them as you need. If you keep all your notes in a notebook, you will find it frustrating having to keep flipping back and forth between notes and you will not be able to have all of your notes in front of you, spread out.

Equally, investing in some dividers for your folder is useful. Most commonly, students use these to divide up by the different topics or their different teachers. This is fine, but think about having a section where you can put all of your marked practice work together too. It does not matter what the topic of an essay is, the feedback that you received on it will be useful when you write essays on other topics, and having them all together will encourage you to refer to them more often.

You may also want to consider why you are bringing every note you ever made in politics to every lesson. You could invest in a 'working file' which you carry every day. This might be a single ring-binder with a number of dividers for all of your subjects and teachers. Keep the most recent 2–3 weeks' worth of work in here. Once it gets older than this, have a subject-specific lever arch file at home, and file the work in here. This also means if you ever lose your bag, you will not lose every piece of work too.

Finally, think about how you are going to keep track of your notes. You may want to colour code the top right-hand the corner of your notes for a quick way to identify topics, or create a contents page for your folder. The next chapter will give you advice on how to take notes effectively too.

If you are not organised from the outset, you will find it far more challenging when you come to write essays, revise or find where the gaps in your knowledge are. To achieve the top marks, you would be better placed spending your time working on an essay, rather than hunting for notes that you think you made a few weeks ago.

> **! Common pitfall**
>
> Students who do not look after and organise their notes often find too late that it is a vital skill. Doing so will allow you more time to focus on the more important skills of reading and writing.

Activity

Decide how you are going to get yourself organised for study...and do it! This sounds like an easy task, and therefore too many students neglect to actually do it...so do it now.

The bottom line

> - AO1 knowledge and understanding, AO2 analysis and AO3 evaluation are all required to achieve tops marks.
> - Analysis and evaluation have some overlap, but analysis breaks down one concept and evaluation shows its relationship to the question.
> - The key question for analysis is 'why?', and for evaluation it is 'so what?'
> - It is necessary to answer (some) questions with a broader view than a single topic or interpretation; this is synopticity.
> - You need to get organised before you start your study; trying to do so afterwards is too late and time-consuming.

2 Political reading and note-taking

The biggest single thing that will help you develop your writing skills is reading. This does not mean just reading political books (although that is recommended); rather, you should be reading far more widely. This means **regular** reading of newspapers, academic journals and blogs, as well as books. Too few students read anywhere near enough, and the result of this is that while you may understand the feedback your teacher has given you, you do not actually have the skills to implement it.

It is easy to dismiss this, believing that you already know how to read. However, being able to read effectively and efficiently is quite different, and lots of students do not have these reading skills.

You also need to undertake regular reading in politics as it is a constantly evolving discipline. Textbooks that refer to Cameron being the prime minister or Obama being the president are clearly out of date. Not only will you need to read to gain information about political theory, you will then need to have a good and recent collection of evidence which you can use to support or criticise these theories. For reading in politics to be useful, it needs to be more than just a passive act.

The difference between...

Passive reading	Active reading
In this type of reading, your brain is not particularly engaged. You may read and understand all the words, but you do not think how this relates to what else you know, and take few or no notes. You will probably remember little of this later on.	In this type of reading, you understand the words and ideas of what you are reading, but will also be interested in the wider context — who wrote the text or where it was published, how this links to what you already know, and what new vocabulary you can learn. You will probably write some notes about these thoughts.

If you are reading your textbook or an online news article in a passive way, you will find it difficult to explain later in an essay what you have read or why it was relevant. Below, you will find techniques that will help you to ensure that what you read is relevant and this will help you become an active reader.

Reading techniques

There are three main reading techniques that you will need to get you started in your study of politics — skimming, scanning and active. These are all core reading techniques that will allow you to develop your AO1 knowledge and understanding of politics. Before undertaking any reading, you should ensure you know what you are trying to achieve. For example, are you reading your textbook to gain new knowledge of a process you have not learnt yet, or are you reading a news article for a specific example that you need to use in an essay? Knowing this before you begin is important, otherwise you end up reading a lot but gaining very little from it. You are likely to work through these different types of reading, from skim-reading through to critical reading if that is appropriate (see Figure 2.1).

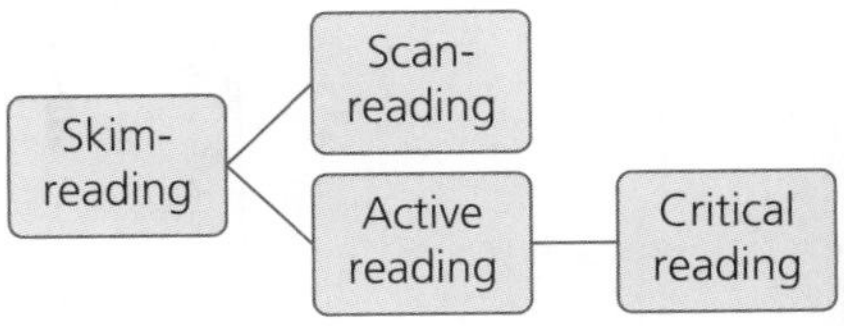

Figure 2.1 Working through the different types of reading

> ## ! Common pitfall
>
> Too many students think reading more is better. You might read lots but if you are a passive reader, you are working hard, not smart. Reading well (actively) is far more important, and indeed more tiring. If you have been 'reading' for hours yet are not feeling tired, you probably have not been reading effectively.

Skim-reading

Skim-reading is a core skill. However, understanding it is crucial to ensuring that what you read is actually relevant to your study. When you skim-read, you are looking to gain an understanding of what the general idea of the text is, but not the detail, so that you can decide whether reading it properly will actually help you to achieve your goal. You must therefore first of all know roughly what topic you are reading about before you begin.

Skim-reading involves:

→ looking for headings and sub-headings
→ identifying key words (which may be in bold or italics)
→ reading the opening paragraph
→ in a longer piece, reading the opening and closing lines of each paragraph
→ looking at pictures, charts, graphs or other data

This should give you a clear idea of what the whole article, chapter or book is about, from which you can decide if further reading is needed or if the piece is not useful.

> ## ! Common pitfall
>
> Students too often skim-read as their only form of reading, especially with smart phones displaying so little of a story on the screen. Learn that skim-reading is usually just the first step to give you the gist of a story or a chapter.

> ## Activity
>
> Skim-read the chapter of your textbook that is relevant to your current topic of study in class. Doing so will help you gain a better overview of the topic and help you to place more detailed information into a broader picture.

Scan-reading

Scan reading is also a core skill, but one you might need if you are looking for specific information or evidence for an essay you are writing. You may need an example to help support a specific point that you are making, but you already understand all the theory so you do not want to read a whole chapter or article. In this case, you would first skim-read the article to ensure it is likely to contain the information you want. Then you should go back to the beginning and scan the article for the information you are looking for:

→ You might look for capital letters (names of politicians, titles or places).

→ You might look for numbers (dates, statistics).

→ You might look for a specific word or phrase.

In order to scan-read, you must therefore know **exactly** what you are looking for before you begin.

! Common pitfall

Do not think that a name, date or event is an 'example'. A good example will be explained more fully and then applied to the question.

Active reading

Active reading is the final core reading skill and it is vital to your success as a student. It is reading but with a purpose. This is a development of skim-reading, when you were reading only to find out the overview; you are now reading to understand. You will most likely be actively reading your textbook, or other core texts that your teacher gives you, as this is where you will be able to get the basic understanding of the new theories and concepts that you are studying. For active reading to be most effective, you will be taking notes as you are reading (advice on which is given in the next section).

If you are reading actively, you will be thinking too. This may mean that you:

→ read a section, and then look away from your textbook and test yourself to see what you can remember

→ highlight and underline key points and arguments

→ summarise and re-phrase the reading into notes using your own words or diagrams

→ make a glossary of new or important vocabulary

→ try to draw links from your reading to what you already know

! Common pitfall

Reading on its own is not effective for your studies and over time you are likely to forget much of what you have read. Instead, active reading strategies and note-taking should help you to make links to your studies and make reading a good use of your time.

Activity

Using a recent news story that is relevant to your current topic of study, have a go at active reading. If you are struggling, you can always find a story at www.lgspolitics.wordpress.com

Understanding difficult passages

Your textbook, like this book, will have been written with A-level students in mind. However, other reading, especially academic books and journal articles, can often be written in more complex language. If you have found a useful article, but have come across words or sentences that you do not understand, do not simply ignore them (see example 2.1 on page 18).

Annotated example 2.1

When you read, you gain understanding not from individual words, but from sentences and paragraphs. Start by trying to read the whole paragraph in one go to see if it makes sense overall.

Look up words that you might not understand in a dictionary, for example 'Faustian' — a politics dictionary can be particularly helpful for this.

Republicans in Congress should be braver

The pact between Republicans in Congress and the president always looked more than a bit Faustian. Many Republican lawmakers decided to cheerlead for a president who won the nomination by running against their party, in the expectation that he would then help them pass the laws they wanted. They were misinformed. The collapse of healthcare legislation has shown that, despite his boasts, the president is hardly a master-dealmaker who can help Republicans get bills through Congress. The defenestration of Reince Priebus, Sean Spicer and the short-lived Anthony Scaramucci shows that he also has a habit of rewarding even his most loyal defenders with public humiliation.

The collapse of healthcare legislation is a huge topic, for which it is difficult to find a simple explanation. But your teacher may be able to help here.

Are there any clues in this sentence that help explain meaning? In this case, 'defenestration' seems to be linked to some form of 'humiliation'. If there are such clues, this might give you enough understanding to move on and you might not need to understand everything.

Can you break this sentence down into smaller chunks? You might even be able to rewrite the sentence. For example:

● 'Republican lawmakers' = Republican Congressmen

● 'cheerlead' = support

● 'won the nomination by running against their party' = Trump's primary campaign criticised the traditional Republican Party

● 'he would then help them' — Trump would help the Congressmen

You could rewrite the sentence as 'Republican Congressmen supported Trump's almost anti-Republican primary campaign, expecting to gain his support for their bills.'

Source: 'Republicans in Congress should be braver', 3 August 2017, *The Economist*.

Take it further

How you write is crucial to high attainment, now and at university. Read the following online article published by *Business Insider* to develop your knowledge about sentence structure:

'Why this sentence is hard to understand' http://uk.businessinsider.com/why-this-sentence-is-hard-to-understand-2015-3?r=US&IR=T

 Exam tip

While you may come across long, complex sentences in academic writing, you should always try and keep your sentences short. It reads better and will usually help your work make more sense.

Types of reading in action

Annotated example 2.2

Imagine you are conducting some reading for an essay that discusses how powerful the vice president of the USA actually is.

This is what the different types of reading might identify within this article (information about 'critical reading' is given on pages 29–30).

The vice president casts a tie-breaking vote in the Senate

Mike Pence cast a historic vote just over 2 weeks into Trump's presidency — he cast the tie-breaking vote in the Senate to confirm a cabinet nominee. While Vice President Biden never had to exercise this constitutional power in his 8 years, it is not uncommon for a vice president to have to. However it has never been done before to confirm a cabinet nominee.

Trying to fill the cabinet

First, it demonstrates the importance a vice president can have. In this case, it allowed the Trump administration to continue filling the cabinet, something they have been struggling to do with Congress only slowly confirming nominees. In the event of a 50–50 tie in the Senate, the vice president can break the deadlock and is likely to do so in favour of the president; in this case Pence's vote confirmed De Vos as Education Secretary.

It is also a useful example when examining factors that a president may consider when nominating someone. Democrats have accused De Vos of having no educational experience which is usually a key factor a president will look at when nominating; she has however been a considerable donor to the Republican Party which makes her a good example of the other considerations a president might have in filling these posts.

Skim-reading: the piece is about one vote in the Senate.

Skim-reading: Pence voted to confirm a cabinet member; this is unusual.

Critical reading: Trump has apparently been struggling to fill the cabinet — what evidence is there? What evidence is there about vice presidents voting the way their president wants?

Active reading: the case of Betsy DeVos is especially important as Trump has been struggling to fill his cabinet.

Critical reading: the key argument is that this is an unusual occurrence — why? What about other vice presidents?

Active reading: the vice president can break a tie in the Senate, therefore has some power. Vote was 'historic' because it has never happened before.

Scan-reading: Pence voted to confirm De Vos as Education Secretary in a Senate tie. Biden never used this power; no vice president has for a cabinet member.

Scan-reading: De Vos was approved. A vice president is likely to vote with his president.

The Constitution and the power of Congress

Equally, the role of the Congress and the Constitution is crucial in this example. Congress has the right to approve or reject nominees, but this remains a reactive power — they can only act once the president has nominated. The role of Congress and its ability to act is frequently criticised due to the slow nature of what it does — in this case the Democrats staged a 24-hour walk out in order to try and persuade just one more Republican to vote against De Vos, and avoid the need for Pence to cast a tie-breaker. This suggests the role of parties within Congress remains a prominent one and is clearly one of the factors that Congressmen consider when voting.

On the other hand, it is clearly not the only factor — two Republicans voted against De Vos. This would be great when writing an essay about party factions and ideology as these senators are both more centrist within their party (Collins and Murkowski) and suggest other factors may have influenced their vote. Equally, the fact that Congress is being so slow at confirming Trump's nominees, despite his rhetoric and tweeting, suggests Congress does have power to exercise, even over a newly elected president.

An historic vote

Finally, as this is the first time in history that this kind of tie-breaking vote has been cast, students should be wary of placing too much emphasis on it. It does of course show the power that a vice president can have, but as this has been exercised just once during a cabinet nominee vote (in over 200 years), this suggests that it is, at least in terms of frequency, not an important power for the vice president.

Adapted from LGS Politics Blog, 8 February 2017: https://lgspolitics.wordpress.com/2017/02/08/tie-breaking-pence/

Skim-reading: the confirmation role is normally that of Congress.

Critical reading: how many times, and for what appointments, have other tie-breaking votes needed to be cast?

Active reading: Congress can try and prevent this vice presidential power by ensuring there is no tie in the Senate, which lessens the vice president's importance.

Skim-reading: this was a unique occurrence.

Critical reading: if it has never happened before, why now? How strong is the nominee, and how popular is the president?

Critical reading: this is an article written for A-level students.

Active reading: this has happened only once in over 200 years and therefore is both a great example and unlikely to be repeated.

The points made here are not exhaustive, but they should give you a good idea of the reading skills in action. You might have made different points for each reading skill and missed ones listed here — but the crucial point is that you understood what you were doing.

(See pages 29–30 for more information on the skill of critical reading.)

Knowing what to read

Reading is an expected part of A-level study, and crucial in a current-affairs-based subject like politics. To achieve the top grades, do not expect to be set specific reading by your teacher; instead go and find something for yourself. However, you must be aware of what makes something worth reading.

Textbooks

While the internet is a great resource, you are likely to have been given a textbook and this should be the first place you look. This is because your textbook is likely to have been written specifically for your course and is pitched at the right reading level for A-level students. Also, your textbook is a 'reliable source' — that is, you know who the author and publisher is, and it will have been proofread and checked for accuracy. This is not a always true for the internet.

Take it further

Useful A-level textbooks

- Lynch, P., Fairclough, P. and Cooper, T. (2017) *UK Government and Politics for AS/A-level*, 5th edn, Hodder Education.
- McNaughton, N. (2017) *Edexcel UK Government and Politics for AS/A-level,* 5th edn, Hodder Education.
- Heywood, A. (2017) *Essentials of UK Politics*, 4th edn, Palgrave.
- Goodlad, G. and Mitchell, A. (2017) *Edexcel GCE Politics AS and A-Level*, Pearson Education.
- McNaughton, N. and Kelly, R. (2017) *Political Ideas for A-level: Liberalism, Conservatism, Socialism, Feminism, Anarchism*, Hodder Education.
- McNaughton, N. and Kelly, R. (2017) *Political Ideas for A-level: Liberalism, Conservatism, Socialism, Nationalism, Multiculturalism and Ecologism*, Hodder Education.
- Bennett, A. (2017) *US Government and Politics for A-level*, 5th edn, Hodder Education.
- Murphy, R., Jefferies, J. and Gadsby, J. (2017) *Global Politics for A-level,* Hodder Education.

When reading your textbook, it is useful to know what your course specification is so that you are able to read actively — so that you know what the purpose of your reading is. Aim to read the chapters that are relevant to what you are currently studying, rather than the whole book all at once, so that you do not become a passive reader. Taking notes as you read is also important.

Note-taking

Taking notes on what you read and in your lessons is a required skill of an A-level student. It should ensure that you are thinking about what you are hearing or reading, and it will mean that you have information to revise from at the end of your course. Note-taking must be done properly to be useful, however, and too often students simply copy out vast chunks of text. This is a passive way of taking notes and although you might gain some knowledge (AO1) from it, you will probably not retain it. Certainly, it does not help in developing your analytical and evaluation skills.

What should I note?

Whether you are making notes from your reading, or in your lesson, what you note will depend on one key question — is it important? Things that are likely to be important are:

→ ideas, concepts or evidence that is new to you
→ a general overview of the 'big' ideas
→ questions regarding things that you are unsure about

What you definitely should not be noting is everything. If you know there is information in your textbook that you have already noted, there is no need to note it twice. If it is information that you are unlikely ever to use again, there is little value in noting it. If the information has little or no relevance to your course, there is no point in noting it.

When noting from reading especially, it is important that you ensure the detail is sufficient. The key reason to note anything is so that you do not have to return to the original source later on. If your notes are vague, or make reference to the name of an example but with no detail, and you do have to go back to the original source, then you should question why you actually wrote any notes in the first place — they were clearly not effective.

Bibliographic detail

In an exam you would not be required to cite where you got your information from. However, in longer academic essays, perhaps for an essay competition or at university, you will be expected to show your sources.

Whenever you begin to note from a source, the very first thing you should record at the top of the page is the key bibliographical information of your source. Commonly, you should try and identify:

→ author
→ title (including sub-titles or edition number)
→ date published
→ publisher
→ place of publication

Obviously, for internet sources or newspaper and magazine articles, this is more difficult. Each university will have its own way of citing references but in short, you want whoever is reading your work to

---

! Common pitfall

Too many students try to write down everything they read or hear. This is problematic as you are unlikely to be able to do so, but by trying to you have become a passive learner. Instead of trying to understand and question what you are reading or hearing, you are just transcribing. This is not a core skill.

! Common pitfall

When noting from reading, do not simply note what is in the article or book. It is only useful to you if it supports or challenges something you are learning. Therefore you should show how what you are noting links to a specific bit, or bits, of your course.

! Common pitfall

When noting from reading, make sure that you also note where you found the information — the book, website, author, publication date and so on. This will be an absolute requirement at university and it is a good habit to get into now. It will help you when analysing your notes.

---

be able to get back to the exact article you are reading in case they want to check your work. This will also be helpful for you as it means you can always come back at a later date and know exactly what you were reading.

For magazines and newspapers, the title of the article and the title of the magazine should be recorded. For internet sources, record the long hyperlink. Crucially, you should also record the date you accessed an internet source. News outlets have a tendency to edit and update their articles, so a quote that you originally wrote down may disappear over time. This is more easily explained if you can show when you accessed the information.

Note-taking in lessons and lectures

In your lessons, it is just as important not to try and note everything your teacher says. Firstly, this is still very passive and does not mean you understandly it. Secondly, in the classroom you have an opportunity to engage in debate, ask questions and try and form links between information. The more you take part in these kinds of activities, the greater understanding you will develop. Therefore, you must be selective about what you are noting in lessons.

How should I note?

Producing notes is a personal thing and you will need to work on creating your own style — one that you understand and is useful for you. Many students rely on highlighting; this is far from ideal. You may end up with a colourful page but will remember and understand little of what you have actually read. Instead, you should aim to write your own notes. How you lay them out — on lined paper, as a spider diagram, on index cards, on a laptop — is up to you. But there are some simple rules that will make this easier:

→ Always use your own words rather than copying text. This will allow you to be selective and more concise — you are unlikely to remember huge chunks of copied text as copying is not an active form of reading.

→ Try to note more than just facts. If the author has a viewpoint or an argument, outline this too. Your notes will form the foundation for your analysis and evaluation.

→ Be selective — only you can judge what is actually worth noting.

→ Make sure that any quotes are clearly marked in quotation marks.

→ Remember that your notes are for you — spelling, grammar, punctuation and layout are all unimportant as long as you can understand them. No one else is going to read your notes so they only need to make sense to you.

→ Have two colours for noting — one colour for quotes or summaries from your reading, and one for your thoughts on how this links to your studies, your own knowledge or the questions it raises for you.

> **! Common pitfall**
>
> Do you actually need to copy down from a presentation that your teacher is giving you? If it is available on your school's VLE or online, then you could download it before or after your lesson and annotate it, rather than spending valuable time merely copying off the board.

> **! Common pitfall**
>
> Avoid highlighting if possible. Not only do you remember little of what you have highlighted, but most students do not even revisit highlighted work. Being a picky noter is far more effective.

> **! Common pitfall**
>
> Avoid copying, especially anything more than a few words in quotation marks. You are less likely to remember what you have copied and it is time-consuming. Write in your own words and be concise.

Take it further

- For essay competitions, or for universities, when you reference something you have read in an essay, you must show not only where it came from but also the page number. Get in the habit of writing page numbers in the margin next to the notes you make from that page.
- Most universities have advice about reading and note-taking on their websites. Look at the advice offered by some of the universities that you may be considering applying to and try to incorporate their advice into your own note-taking.

Make sure that you also organise your notes. Within your notes from just one source, you might use headings, sub-headings, underlining and colours to make your notes clearer. You may choose always to date your work, number the pages or colour-code the top corner of each page by topic. If you are making notes on a computer, make sure that you have your files sorted out and that your file names are clear and detailed.

Making your own notes is always preferable as they will then make sense to you. If you are noting in class, however, you might be able to be more collaborative:

→ Could your class set up a Facebook group to share information or help each other when you are stuck?

→ Could you use Google Docs or other web-based software to allow you all to edit one document of notes?

→ Could you use your school's VLE to share ideas, discussions and reading that you have done?

Obviously it is important not simply to 'take' someone else's work. Not only is this effectively plagiarism, but you will learn little from it and therefore will not remember it when it comes to the exam. But, if you can work to help each other out, this is a very sensible and mature approach.

Shorthand and abbreviations

One way in which you can make your notes more concise is by using shorthand. These are symbols that represent words and make it quicker for you to note. They also mean that your notes do not become one massive block of text that you find hard to break down and use later on. Tables 2.1 and 2.2 show some common symbols and political abbreviations that you might find useful. You can add your own to these, but whatever you add, ensure that you can remember them.

> **! Common pitfall**
>
> It is important to review your notes periodically. After a lesson, take some time to go over what you have learnt, fill in any gaps or identify things you actually did not understand. Do not leave this until revision time.

> **! Common pitfall**
>
> Do not shy away from collaborative work. You are competing against the mark scheme, not your friends!

Table 2.1 Shorthand symbols

=	Equals	→	Leads to	i.e.	That is
≠	Does not equal	↳	Leads to	cf.	Compare with/to
>	Greater than	∴	Therefore	w/	With
<	Less than	∵	Because	w/out	Without

Table 2.2 Political abbreviations

Govt.	Government	Pres.	President	Con.	Conservatives
PM	Prime minister	Cong.	Congress	LD	Liberal Democrats
Parl.	Parliament	Dept.	Department	Lab.	Labour
SC	Supreme Court	Sov.	Sovereignty	Reps.	Republicans
Natl.	National	Fem.	Feminism	Dems.	Democrats

How to read beyond the syllabus

Once you have a good foundation of knowledge from your textbook, you should supplement this with information from other sources if you wish to aim for the top grades. Importantly, however, these sources must be reliable and high quality. You must read such sources critically and analytically, taking thoughtful notes rather than simply copying.

Take it further

Most universities offer public access to their libraries. They might not allow you to borrow books, but you can go along and do research at the library. Find your local university and spend a day in its library.

Reliable media

In the sources shown in Table 2.3, you should be able to find political goings-on, such as bills being passed, speeches and national events. You will also be able to find **editorial** and **opinion** pieces. Editorial pieces are unsigned opinions, usually written by the senior staff of a newspaper, which reflect the views of that newspaper. These persuasion pieces of writing are a good place to see examples of AO2 and AO3 skills in action. Opinion pieces are similar, but written by authors who are not necessarily part of the newspaper staff. Both editorials and opinion pieces will help you develop your knowledge and give you examples of using evidence to make a judgement.

Table 2.3 Reliable sources of political information

UK politics	US politics	Global politics
• BBC News • Channel 4 News • *The Week* • The 'broadsheets' (newspapers that focus on more serious analysis of political events than the tabloids; in the UK, these are the *Guardian*, the *Telegraph*, and *The Times*)	• Politico • *The Washington Post* • *New York Times* • Roll Call • *Wall Street Journal*	• Al Jazeera • *Financial Times* • *The Economist*

Take it further

Politics Review is a quarterly magazine produced for A-level politics students. Not only does it contain articles on topics you study, it also includes articles on exam skills and tips. Ask your teacher about subscribing.

! Common pitfall

When using a source, you must make sure it is 'reliable'. Is it a well-known source? Is the author identified? Can you verify any of the facts it claims? Do you know what the purpose of the site is? Does the domain name look sensible? If the answer to any of these is no, dig a little deeper.

Media bias

When using media sources, you must be wary of the viewpoints from which they are written. While high-quality media are reliable, they almost all have a political leaning that can be seen in their writing.

→ Right-leaning media favour a more conservative view, for example the *Telegraph*, *Times*, *Wall Street Journal*, *Financial Times*.

→ Left-leaning media favour a more liberal view, for example the *Guardian*, the BBC, Channel 4 News, *The Washington Post*, *New York Times*.

This does not mean their writing cannot be trusted; rather, it means you should read critically when using these sources.

Twitter

There are other places that can help to keep you up to date with political events, such as Twitter.

Twitter is a brilliant source of information. You can set up your own Twitter account — even one that you only use for your study of politics — and get notifications delivered straight to your phone. There are three main types of useful Twitter feeds for students of politics: those from traditional media sources; those from political figures; and those from schools and colleges.

(1) Twitter feeds from traditional media sources

The BBC, *The Washington Post* and other media sources have their own Twitter feeds. Many of them have dedicated politics feeds. Some of the most useful are shown in Table 2.4.

Table 2.4 Useful Twitter feeds from traditional media sources

UK politics	US politics	Global politics
• House of Commons Library: @commonslibrary • BBC politics: @BBCpolitics • *Guardian* politics: @Gdnpolitics • UCL Constitution Unit: @ConUnit_UCL	• Politico: @politico • *The Atlantic*: @TheAtlantic • *New York Times* politics: @NYTpolitics	• Al Jazeera: @AJEnews • *The Economist*: @TheEconomist • *Financial Times*: @FT

By following some of these media outlets you will be able to access the most up-to-date news. You must, however, do more than simply read the headlines. When a story appears that you think might be useful to your studies, make sure you actually open up the story and read it properly.

! Common pitfall

Too many students believe that bias is 'bad'. Writing can be biased but still present a critical argument, and still provide accurate factual information.

✓ Exam tip

When it comes to revision, it can be difficult to find all of the examples you have looked at on Twitter. Keeping a notebook of the examples you find (with dates and authors) can be useful. Alternatively, if you 'like' tweets that you have found useful, you will find them stored under the 'likes' heading on your profile page. This can help to keep you better organised.

! Common pitfall

The volume of information on Twitter is immense and filtering through it can be daunting. The simplest way to start is to follow only a few, well-selected feeds. Follow only one or two news outlets, a few politicians and a few other feeds. Following everything will just make it more confusing, and often repetitive as many news sites will carry the some story.

(2) Twitter feeds from political figures

Twitter gives you the opportunity to follow political figures themselves and obtain quotes and opinions directly. Following Donald Trump for example (@realDonaldTrump) is useful not only to gain information, but also to gain his view of events that are occurring.

The difference between...

Interesting information	Useful information
There will be lots of news that is interesting. A story might be funny, unusual or embarrassing and therefore make a headline. These sorts of stories are not usually helpful to either analysing or evaluating the political concepts you are learning.	A useful story is one that can help to illustrate, support or challenge the theories you have learnt. Some of these may be headline stories, but some will not be. If you read a story that is an example of something you have learnt in action, this is more likely to be a useful story.
For example: in 2017, Boris Johnson referred to Jeremy Corbyn as a 'mutton-headed old mugwump'. While interesting, there are very few ways in which this comment has any links to your specification.	For example: in 2017, Trump tweeted that he planned to ban transgender people serving in the military. Less reported was the response of his administration, which was that the details of how to do this had not yet been worked out. This is useful when discussing how much power the president alone actually has.

Activity

Go to the political homepage of the BBC News website (www.bbc.co.uk/news/politics) and sort the first five stories you find into 'interesting' and 'useful' using the advice given above.

As a politics student, the information you can gain from political figures themselves is incredibly useful for analysis (AO2) and evaluation (AO3) skills. However, simply knowing the views of a politician is knowledge (AO1). Certainly, you would not write a paragraph in an essay with the views from a tweet in your first line. Instead, it would be evidence that you use when discussing your point.

As the elected representatives and leaders change frequently, it may be more helpful to follow the official accounts of the offices of political figures, rather than the people themselves. Table 2.5 gives some examples.

Annotated example 2.3 shows you how much you can gain from just one tweet.

! Common pitfall

While Twitter and other media are great tools, be wary of what you choose to note. Something that is headline news or trending on Twitter might be exciting or interesting, but actually of little value to your academic study. Make sure you only note information that can be linked to the theories you have studied; if it cannot, it will not be useful.

Table 2.5 Twitter feeds from official offices

UK politics	US politics	Global politics
UK prime minister: @Number10gov	US president: @POTUS	EU Council president: @eucopresident

Annotated example 2.3

Read the tweet below. Whether you have studied US politics or not, what can we infer about:

- The US and Russia?
- Healthcare in the US?
- The president's relationship with Congress?
- The president's power?

Tweet from @realDonaldTrump on 3 August 2017

> Our relationship with Russia is at an all-time &
> very dangerous low. You can thank Congress, the
> same people that can't even give us HCare!

What can we take from this tweet?

- The use of 'our' as the first word is interesting — it is a unifying word and reminds us that Trump is the president of everyone in the USA, not just those who voted for him.
- The use of the phrase 'very dangerous' suggests that the USA's lack of a relationship with Russia is not just unfortunate but could be a problem for the USA. This, coupled with the point above, suggests it will be a problem for every American.
- 'You can thank Congress' suggests that Congress is not acting as Trump would like. Trump uses irony to make this point and it could imply that the relationship between the president and Congress is strained.
- The word 'even' in Trump's comment that Congress 'can't even give us HCare (healthcare)' suggests that he is frustrated by Congress's inaction (regarding 'Repeal and Replace' of Obamacare), and implies that this should have been simple for Congress to do.
- Again, note the use of the word 'us' — Trump is trying to appeal to all Americans as one.
- Comparing the language used about healthcare and Russia suggests that Trump is more concerned over the relationship with Russia — this Russian relationship is 'dangerous' whereas healthcare is blamed on Congress.
- The whole tweet suggests the US president has clear restraints on his power; in this case, Trump wants both a better relationship with Russia and progress on healthcare but has neither yet.

From this, you can then start to consider adding in your own knowledge and linking this to things you have learnt, for example:

- As head of state, the president is usually in charge of foreign affairs, yet as he cannot gain a good relationship with Russia, this suggests there are checks on his power even in this area. This could be coupled with the numerous investigations into Russia's alleged election tampering in 2016.
- The USA has separation of powers enshrined in the Constitution to ensure one branch cannot dominate another. In this instance, these checks and balances mean that while Trump wants healthcare reform, he must work with Congress to achieve it.
- At the time of this tweet, Trump had a Republican majority in both the House of Representatives and the Senate. The collapse of 'Repeal and Replace' suggests that the Republican Party are not acting with unity, because they should have the votes to pass it. This could be a good example when discussing factors that influence voting in Congress.

All of this from a tweet that is just 140 characters long! There are many more points that you could add here, and this kind of activity helps to develop your critical reading and thinking (see below) as well as your synoptic skills.

Activity

Find a tweet from a high-ranking politician in the UK. Conduct the same breakdown as in example 2.3 — what can you infer, and what can you add?

(2) Twitter feeds from schools and colleges

There are a large number of schools and colleges that run their own Twitter feed for their students. These are really useful to follow as it means you do not have to spend so much time trying to work out whether a tweet is actually useful, or whether it is simply interesting. Often, these feeds will retweet the most important stories with some additional information about which bit of your course they are relevant to.

Political information

You can also find specific political information and data on some reliable government websites. These will provide you with evidence that you can analyse to make an argument in your essay. Some of the most useful of these are:

➡ UK parliament: www.parliament.uk
➡ Parliamentary Archives: www.parliament.uk/business/ publications/parliamentary-archives/
➡ Commons Library: www.parliament.uk/commons-library
➡ The White House: www.whitehouse.gov
➡ Congress: www.congress.gov
➡ Open Secrets: www.opensecrets.org

Critical reading

When you read a text critically, you start by using your active reading skill to find out what the text actually says and take some notes about this. Once you have done this, the critical reading skill is used to pose questions not just about the detail and arguments within the text, but also about the purpose of the text. To do this, you are going to add any questions, strengths and weaknesses that you have identified to your notes.

To begin with, once you know what the article is about, review its provenance:

➡ Who wrote it and when?
➡ What was the purpose of writing it?
➡ Who was the intended audience for the piece?

In answering these questions, you need to review whether this has an impact on the piece you have read. It may be that it was written for a left-leaning newspaper, or written to persuade people to vote a certain way. If this is the case, this may pose further questions about what you have just read.

You will then need to look at the notes that you have made from the article and see what questions you can raise about this:

→ Does the evidence presented agree with or contradict what you already know?

→ Are there any limitations to the evidence presented? For example, are there vague phrases like 'most people' or 'some scholars', or is the evidence specific?

→ Does the author interpret the evidence well?

→ Why did the author select the evidence that they did?

→ Do you agree with their interpretation?

This final question is the crucial one. The answer to it does not actually matter: it is your justification of why you agree or disagree with it that is both important and what makes critical reading.

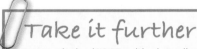

Take it further

Research the 'SQ3R critical reading skill' and see if you can use it to analyse a piece of reading.

Activity

The subject of politics is often satirised in cartoons and understanding these is a great test of your knowledge. Find a recent political cartoon and analyse it using your critical reading skills.

● What is the purpose of the cartoon?

● Who is the intended audience?

● What is the cartoonist's interpretation?

● Do you agree with the cartoonist's interpretation of the situation?

Analysis and evaluation of information

The word 'analysis' can cause students some concern, usually because while they are told to do it, they are not really sure what it means, let alone how to do it.

In analysing a source of information, you need to break down the whole thing and look at the information in smaller parts, identifying within it what is evidence, interpretation and argument. If you do not have much knowledge on a topic, some of your analysis may be identifying things that you need to look up and find out more about.

By contrast, 'evaluation' looks at the piece as a whole and the arguments within it, and asks you to judge whether the piece is reliable, whether the arguments are strong and if the judgements reached are rational.

Annotated example 2.4

Read the below article and try to analyse and evaluate each paragraph, using different colours for each objective. For analysis, think about what you might need to look up or find out more about, what evidence the article offers and if you can make connections with any of your own knowledge (do not worry if you only have a little knowledge right now). For evaluation, look at the argument advanced and identify whether it is well argued and supported or not.

Republicans in Congress should be braver

The bargain they struck with the president is not working for them

3 August 2017

The pact between Republicans in Congress and the president always looked more than a bit Faustian. Many Republican lawmakers decided to cheerlead for a president who won the nomination by running against their party, in the expectation that he would then help them pass the laws they wanted. They were misinformed. The collapse of health-care legislation has shown that, despite his boasts, the president is hardly a master-dealmaker who can help Republicans get bills through Congress. The defenestration of Reince Priebus, Sean Spicer and the short-lived Anthony Scaramucci shows that he also has a habit of rewarding even his most loyal defenders with public humiliation. This pact is indeed like Faust's — but without the enjoyable moments of omnipotence before the reckoning falls due. It is past time for Republicans in Congress to strike a new one.

There are signs that this is happening. After the failure of health-care reform, blocked by a trio of independently minded Republican senators, some Republican legislators have offered to work with Democrats to shore up the Affordable Care Act. Incremental improvements to Obamacare are far more likely to succeed in making Americans healthier than scrapping it and starting afresh.

If Congress can avoid a government shutdown, by approving a budget in September, tax reform will be next on the agenda. Here, Democrats have

Analysis: look up what Faustian means.

Analysis: some did 'cheerlead', but not necessarily willingly, for example Paul Ryan taking a week to endorse Trump.

Evaluation: the two references to Faust imply that Trump is the devil, so the article has a political leaning.

Analysis: which Republican legislators? Where do they sit within the Republican Party spectrum?

Analysis: this might explain Trump's reliance on executive orders.

Evaluation: the suggestion is that the 'independently minded Republicans' are a positive force, implying the other Republicans currently are not.

Evaluation: why would this make Americans healthier?

Analysis: Congress has been routinely avoiding shutdowns since 2013 despite constant threats.

signalled that they may be willing to work with Republicans on a bill to get rid of tax breaks while lowering rates and containing the budget deficit.

Regrettably, the Senate majority leader, Mitch McConnell, has so far rebuffed advances from the other side of the aisle. Perhaps Mr McConnell is hoping that Mr Priebus's successor as chief-of-staff will bring some order to the Trump White House. A former general, John Kelly started well by using his first day to fire the bloviating Mr Scaramucci. Yet he must still cope with the man in the Oval Office who, throughout his business career, has made conflict and infighting a way of life. More likely is that the turbulence will continue and that an angry president will set Republicans in Congress the kind of unreasonable loyalty test he often imposes on his staff. That would be the moment when the Republican Party must show that it stands for more than winning elections.

In Washington being bipartisan is risky and deeply unfashionable. But it is what the country urgently needs.

Evaluation: the 'conflict' is evident from Trump's use of Twitter and rhetoric regarding North Korea. However, he has lasted longer than some expected.

Analysis: Trump has struggled to keep a coherent White House staff with a number of high-profile sackings (some mentioned in paragraph 1), which undermines the importance of the Executive Office of the President of the United States.

Evaluation: this is clearly an anti-Trump piece but it is supplemented with accurate evidence and a clear line of argument from a reputable source. It ignores criticism that Trump has received from Republicans and suggests the party speaks as one.

There is more that can be included here and you might have identified different points, but this should help you see the difference between analysis and evaluation.

Source: 'Republicans in Congress should be braver', 3 August 2017, *The Economist*.

The bottom line

> **Always know what the purpose of any reading is before you begin.**
> **You need to employ a range of reading techniques, which all need practising. Passive reading is time-consuming and ultimately will achieve very little for your studies.**
> **Sources must be identified as reliable and relevant before you undertake more in-depth reading tasks.**
> **Note-taking is a deeply personal thing and you need to develop your own style — the only one to whom your notes need to make sense is you.**
> **Not everything needs noting, especially in lessons — taking part is often more important and certainly more active than writing down everything you hear.**
> **To access the top marks, critical reading and reading widely are absolutely crucial.**

3 Writing a short answer

Writing is a highly personal skill — it is important that you understand that there is no right way to write. The advice below is something you should aim to integrate into your own writing style, not something you should try and copy in every answer. If you try to write like someone else, your work will end up sounding very odd and you will find it very stressful.

Regardless of your exam board, you are going to have to answer some shorter questions which focus on what you have learnt — AO1. But before you even begin to start thinking about how to answer these, you must know how your exam board is going to assess you for each question.

Your exam board

AQA

Table 3.1 shows how the marks are allocated in AQA short-answer questions.

Table 3.1 Mark scheme for AQA short-answer questions

Level	Marks	Command word	AO marks
AS	6	Explain	AO1: 6
AS	12	Analyse, evaluate and compare	AO1: 2 AO2: 6 AO3: 4
A-level	9	Explain and analyse	AO1: 6 AO2: 3

Edexcel

Table 3.2 shows how the marks are allocated in Edexcel short-answer questions.

Table 3.2 Mark scheme for Edexcel short-answer questions

Level	Marks	Command word	AO marks
AS	10	Describe	AO1: 10
	10	Explain (using a source)	AO1: 10
	10	Assess (using two sources)	AO1: 5 AO2: 5
A-level	12	Examine	AO1: 6 AO2: 6

WJEC

If you are doing WJEC politics, make sure you know that AOs are slightly different to AQA and Edexcel:

→ AO1: knowledge and understanding
→ AO2: apply and interpret
→ AO3: analyse and evaluate

Additionally, the 24-mark source question in Papers 3 and 4 requires the same skills as outlined in this chapter but your answer is likely to be longer than the recommended three paragraphs.

Table 3.3 Mark scheme for WJEC short-answer questions

Paper	Marks	Command word	AO marks
Papers 1 and 2	6	Varies	AO1: 6
	24 (comparing sources)	Varies	AO1: 8 AO2: 16
Papers 3 and 4	16	Varies	AO1: 4 AO2: 12

Writing short, factual answers

Command words

In order to maximise your marks in short essays, you must understand the common command words for these types of questions. A command word is the word or phrase that tells you what the question wants you to do.

As short-answer questions tend to focus more heavily on the AO1 skill, the command words will most likely want you to display the knowledge that you have learnt. Most commonly, short-answer commands are words such as 'describe' or 'explain'. If a question has marks for more than one AO, the command words will require you to do more than just show your knowledge. In this case, you will see command words such as 'examine', 'analyse' or 'assess'. Table 3.4 lists examples of common command words.

Table 3.4 Common command words in short-answer questions

Command word	AO it is linked to	What you need to do
Analyse	AO1, AO2	Break down a concept into parts. How do the different parts relate to one another?
Assess	AO1, AO2	In what ways can the concept be defended or attacked? What final judgement can be reached about a concept and why?
Compare	AO1, AO2	What are the similarities and differences between these arguments or sources?
Describe	AO1	What are the main features (what it looks like) and the main functions (what it does) of a concept?
Examine	AO1, AO2	What are the key terms and knowledge relevant to the concept? What is the importance or extent of each point?
Explain	AO1	What is the concept and how or why does it occur?

> **! Common pitfall**
>
> Too many students ignore the whole question. You must read every word of the question and ensure that you are answering what you have been asked, rather than simply looking at the topic and writing everything you know about it.

It should be clear from the table that you must do more than simply regurgitate your textbook — you need to answer the question you have been set.

Deconstructing the question

Most short-answer questions share a common structure.

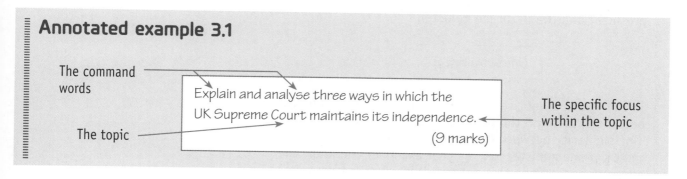

Annotated example 3.1

The command words ———

The topic ———

Explain and analyse three ways in which the UK Supreme Court maintains its independence.

(9 marks)

The specific focus within the topic

Identifying the parts of the question before you start to write is important. It will help to ensure that everything you write is relevant and can gain you marks. You should also find it easier to keep to the timings and not write too much. In the example given, the question only asks about the *independence* of the UK Supreme Court. Therefore, any points that you make about its neutrality may be accurate, but are completely irrelevant to this question and therefore are not worth any marks.

> **✓ Exam tip**
>
> Ensure you have a coloured pen or highlighter handy in the exam. Use this to highlight the command words, topic and focus in a question before you begin. This will help to keep you focused.

Do not be put off if some questions deviate from this pattern. It is not possible to predict exactly how every question will be phrased. As long as you take the time before you begin writing to break down the question, making sure you know exactly what it is asking, you will be on the right track.

Structuring short answers

For A-level Politics, most short-answer questions should be answered in between 10 and 20 minutes. You should aim to write three developed paragraphs, each paragraph consisting of a separate point. (See Chapter 5 for more information on timing in your exam.)

It is crucial that you know roughly how much you can write in this time. There is little point handing in a homework essay to your teacher that is five pages long if you can only write one-and-a-half in timed exam conditions. Rather, you need to know how much you can write in the time allowed, and work to ensure that every one of the words you write helps you gain marks for that question.

Introductions and conclusions are not necessary for short-answer questions, so simply do not include them. They add little, if anything, to your answer and consume valuable time, of which you have little. Instead, you should get straight into the answer. A simple way of doing this is by rewording part of the question.

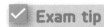

Exam tip

Unless your teacher requires work to be typed or you are allowed to use a laptop in the exam, **always** handwrite your answers. Your exams are handwritten and you need plenty of practice in writing at speed.

Annotated example 3.2

Examine the similarities between the powers of the US president and the UK prime minister.

> One similarity is...

In this example, notice that only part of the question has been used to begin the paragraph. There is no need to write, 'One similarity between the powers of the US president and the UK prime minister is...' as your examiner will know the question and writing this out in full is very time-consuming.

Take it further

Be aware that this style of writing is suitable only for exam conditions where time is precious. If you are writing for essay competitions or for university, you will need to ensure you write in completely full sentences.

Structuring a paragraph

Annotated example 3.3

Examine the factors that affect how members of the US House of Representatives and the UK House of Commons vote.

(12 marks, Edexcel)

From the outset, the focus of this paragraph is clear.

This sentence clearly explains why a representative may be influenced by their party and draws similarities between the US and UK.

This is the beginning of comparative analysis, giving clear explanations of why the party can be more important in the UK.

Words such as 'nonetheless', 'yet', 'while', 'despite this', and so on show both comparison and judgement. Used well, they help to show you are analysing rather than simply describing.

> One factor is the party that the elected representative belongs to. Parties in the US and UK provide electoral support to representatives and expect voting loyalty in return. In both countries, therefore, party-line voting is very common. Even controversial policies like the repeal of Obamacare and Brexit passed with reasonable ease with a high level of party-line voting. As representatives can choose the party they join, they should have a shared ideology with their party, meaning they usually willingly vote with them. This is more important in the UK where the party discipline is stronger. By 'removing the whip', an MP is effectively removed from their party, affecting their re-election chances and the roles they can hold in parliament. Comparatively, the use of primaries means US parties are comparatively less powerful as they cannot deselect candidates, meaning party discipline is weaker. Nonetheless, successful rebellions in both countries are reasonably uncommon, suggesting the importance of party loyalty in voting.

Using political terminology shows that you understand what you have been asked. Common terms like 'elected representative' do not need explaining, provided you are using them correctly.

The examples given in this sentence are important. They have been picked to show that parties are so important they have been able to pass legislation that has caused national controversy.

This student has shown analytical thought by suggesting that while there is a difference, it should not be exaggerated.

There is a lot of information packed into this one paragraph. It is important that you develop the point you are making, for example explaining key terms and showing how and why they are important, rather than listing several factors but only in descriptive terms.

A good rule of thumb to begin with is to follow the P-E-A approach:

P — point

E — explanation and example

A — application to the question

Point

You should identify the point of your paragraph in your opening sentence — it should be clear in your first line what it is that your paragraph is going to be about. If you are able to use political vocabulary in doing this, it demonstrates focus on the question and understanding of the subject in one line. Your point should really only be one sentence.

Explanation and example

Once you have outlined your point, you must explain what it means. This should take up a little over half of your paragraph. You must try to explain 'how' and 'why'. This means that for the point you have given, *how* does it do something and *why* does it do something. In example 3.3, the student explains how the party affects voting (through the whip) and why the party has an impact on voting (because it affects the future electoral chances of a representative).

The difference between...

AO1 consists of both knowledge and understanding. It is important to recognise that these are different skills, but interrelated.

Knowledge	Understanding
Knowledge is having information. You may have learnt this information from your textbook, teacher or your own reading.	Understanding is being able to develop and explain the meaning of your knowledge, placing it in context.
For example, you might know that parliament is sovereign in the UK.	For example, you might understand that sovereignty means that parliament is theoretically the source of all political power in the UK, so it can make or unmake any law.
In short — FACTS.	In short — MEANING.
These exist together!	

Examples can be helpful when you are explaining, and you should try to make sure your examples are 'sandwiched' in the middle of your paragraph and are also explained. Examples are important as they not only support your point, but show that the theory you are writing about also occurs in reality. In example 3.3, the passing of 'controversial' legislation is used as a specific example to show that even in these circumstances parties have been able to rely enough on their members to get legislation through. It is important to pick a relevant example that helps to develop the point you are trying to make.

Application to the question (or analysis)

Application is where you use what you have written to address the specifics of your question directly. This is simply another way to understand 'analysis'. For short-answer questions, the application will probably take up a little under half of your paragraph. In example 3.3, the student was asked to 'examine'. To answer this question fully, they should look at the extent of the similarity or difference between the US and UK, analysing the importance of the point. In this case, the student identifies a difference and judges the importance of this difference, and identifies a similarity, before analysing which of these is more important.

Figure 3.1 shows how the P-E-A structure can be used. Use this as a guide for the rough proportions that each of these skills will take up in a handwritten paragraph. As you develop your writing style, the colours will be more mixed up.

> **! Common pitfall**
>
> Examples are not names and dates — too often, students give examples that are nothing more than a name drop. You must ensure that your examples are sufficiently explained to show that you know what you are talking about and to help you demonstrate the relevance and importance of your example. (See also 'Using evidence' below.)

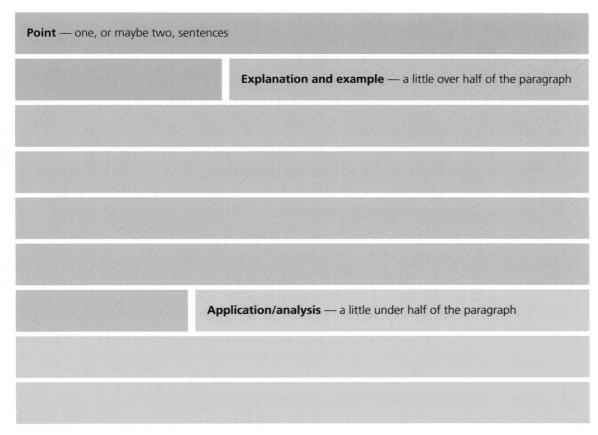

Figure 3.1 Guide to the P-E-A structure

Point — one, or maybe two, sentences

Explanation and example — a little over half of the paragraph

Application/analysis — a little under half of the paragraph

! Common pitfall

Rewording and repeating the question is not application.

✓ Exam tip

One way to begin your application is to reword the question and follow it with the word, 'because'. In Annotated example 3.3, 'This suggests that the party is an important factor in voting because…'.

Activity

Find a short answer that you have already completed and see if you can colour-code the point, explanation and example, and analysis in three different colours. Have you got the balance about right?

Developing your paragraph

The P-E-A structure is a good way to start learning how to structure your paragraph successfully and ensures that you cover everything necessary to gain marks. Once you become comfortable with this, however, you can look to develop your work away from a rigid structure into something more flowing.

Annotated example 3.4

Examine the factors that affect how members of the US House of Representatives and the UK House of Commons vote.

(12 marks)

This answer uses the same point as in example 3.3, but the explanation and application are more blended.

The paragraph still has a clear point.

One factor is the party that the elected representative belongs to. Parties in the US and UK both have discipline structures to encourage voting loyalty from their party members. This is more important in the UK where the party is able to 'remove the whip', effectively removing an MP from their party and affecting their re-election chances and the roles they can hold in parliament. Comparatively, representatives in the US are selected through primaries in their constituency, which reduces the power of the party. In 2017, MP Anne Morris was suspended from the Conservative Party over her use of a racial slur in 2017, yet when more than 25 Republicans voted against the re-election of the incumbent Republican Speaker, they faced few repercussions. Nonetheless, as representatives can choose the party they join, their shared ideology will mean they commonly vote with their party and rebellions are reasonably uncommon in both countries, with even controversial legislation such as the repeal of Obamacare and Brexit passing with reasonable ease and levels of party support.

The application begins much sooner in this paragraph.

The comparative example illustrates the difference.

The student has explained a second, linked reason for party loyalty, before applying it to the question by highlighting a similarity rather than a difference.

Activity

As before, colour-code this paragraph to show the point, explanation and example, and analysis. You should be able to see the development in writing style from example 3.3 to this example.

You can also develop your paragraphs by trying to demonstrate links between the points you are making.

Annotated example 3.5

Adding the following final sentence to the paragraph in example 3.4 allows the answer to flow naturally on to the next point:

> *Given that constituents often make their voting choice by the party of each candidate, the constituents themselves also influence voting behaviour.*

Using evidence

Students of politics often have the word 'example' or 'evidence' drummed into them, and yet too often students do not use evidence effectively. For evidence to be worthwhile in your paragraph, it should not simply repeat the theoretical point or explanation that you have made. Instead, you should pick your evidence carefully to illustrate why the point you have made is important.

This means your examples must be well detailed, without simply telling a story.

Take it further

Read the article, 'How to write in 700 easy lessons' by Richard Bausch. This article puts all advice on writing in context and encourages you to develop your own style:

www.theatlantic.com/magazine/archive/2010/08/how-to-write-in-700-easy-lessons/308043

The difference between...

Explain and analyse three limits to the power of the prime minister.

(9 marks, AQA)

Poor use of evidence	Good use of evidence
One limit on the power of the prime minister is the majority they have in the House of Commons, for example Theresa May. A small majority means prime ministers are weaker.	One limit of the power of the prime minister is the majority they have in the House of Commons. Theresa May 'won' the 2017 general election but did not gain an overall majority, meaning she did not have a Commons majority to rely on to pass legislation. As a result, her plans for grammar school expansion had to be abandoned, as losing this vote would have been incredibly embarrassing.
Expert comment: the student has not actually given an example — they have given a name. There is no explanation of why they chose Theresa May or how it has anything to do with what they have written or the question.	*Expert comment: the student has not simply told the story of the 2017 election. Instead, they have focused only on the bit of the election that is relevant to their writing (that May did not win a majority) and they have explained the impact of that on her power.*

Using examples is important in politics. It helps to show that what should happen in theory, does or does not happen in reality. For example, while Parliament is sovereign in theory, there are lots of examples that could be used of how threats are posed to this power in reality — devolution, the EU, the Supreme Court, referendums, and so on. Examples allow you to compare theory and reality and show whether or not political theory works as expected or is effective.

A simple way to begin to develop this skill is always to try to explain why you picked a specific piece of evidence. For example, why did you choose to write about Thatcher, not Blair or May? Why did you write about *Citizens United v FEC* rather than *McCutcheon v FEC*? This may be because the example you have chosen was the last time that something occurred, because it was controversial or unique, because it continued a trend, or because it demonstrates change over time. All of these explanations show that you are using your evidence, rather than simply describing it.

How to include examples

There are some simple guidelines to help you include examples effectively:

→ **Examples should usually be in the middle of a paragraph.** If you end a paragraph on an example, you have probably not shown why it is useful or analysed what it shows.

→ **Avoid writing 'e.g.'** It is far too easy to follow 'e.g.' with just a name or date, which is a poor use of examples. If you write 'for example' instead, you are much more likely to write a full sentence after it. Better still, in most cases if you delete 'for example' from the beginning of a sentence, it still makes sense and flows much more maturely. See the 'Good use of evidence' paragraph on page 41 for an example.

→ **Pick only one example, and explain why you picked it.** Usually, you will pick an example because it is the most infamous, significant, common or unique occurrence, but in explaining why you decided to write about it, you are showing analytical skill.

→ **Put your example in context.** By explaining the circumstances surrounding your example, you demonstrate its importance. In the 'Good use of evidence' paragraph, it was not losing the election alone that forced May to drop her grammar school policy; it was the consequence that she could not guarantee to win the vote in the Commons.

Brief analysis

Short answers need to have some analysis in them too. All exam boards have marks available for AO2 in at least some of their short-answer questions, so descriptive writing alone is not an option. While analysis only needs to be brief in short answers, students often struggle to understand exactly what it is they have to do. In short, for each point you are making, you should ensure that you are showing how and why something works, and try to show its importance.

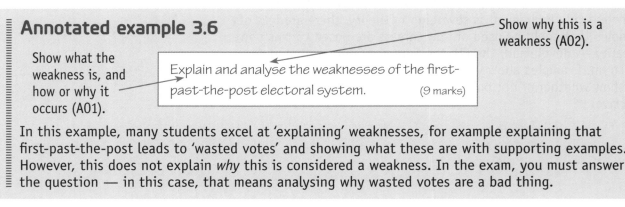

Annotated example 3.6

Show what the weakness is, and how or why it occurs (A01).

Explain and analyse the weaknesses of the first-past-the-post electoral system. (9 marks)

Show why this is a weakness (A02).

In this example, many students excel at 'explaining' weaknesses, for example explaining that first-past-the-post leads to 'wasted votes' and showing what these are with supporting examples. However, this does not explain *why* this is considered a weakness. In the exam, you must answer the question — in this case, that means analysing why wasted votes are a bad thing.

Aiming for an A in A-level Politics

The difference between...

Limited analysis	Good analysis
First-past-the-post (FPTP) leads to 'wasted votes'. These are votes that had no impact on the ultimate outcome of an election, effectively being discarded. As FPTP is a winner-takes-all system, any votes cast for a losing candidate in a constituency gain nothing. In Loughborough, Nicky Morgan represents the whole constituency, yet 50.5% of voters in 2017 voted for another candidate. As half of votes in this constituency were wasted, it is clear that FPTP is flawed.	First-past-the-post (FPTP) leads to 'wasted votes'. These are votes that had no impact on the ultimate outcome of an election, effectively being discarded. As FPTP is a winner-takes-all system, any votes cast for a losing candidate in a constituency gain nothing. In Loughborough, Nicky Morgan represents the whole constituency, yet 50.5% of voters in 2017 voted for another candidate. As a liberal democracy, the UK's universal suffrage operates on a 'one man, one vote' principle. In this example and in FPTP more generally, a large number of the votes cast in an election have no impact, meaning it undermines this principle.
Expert comment: this example implies that wasted votes are a weakness but does not expressly show why.	*Expert comment: this example explains what wasted votes are with a worked example (AO1), but in the two final sentences it shows the relationship between the FPTP election and the UK, identifying specifically why wasted votes are a weakness.*

If you are unsure how to analyse the point that you have made, there are some useful questions you can try to answer:

→ Why is your point a strength?

→ Why is your point a weakness?

→ Why does a similarity or difference exist?

→ What is the impact or consequence of your point?

→ Why is your point important?

(See Chapter 4 for more on developing analysis.)

For all of these questions, you can reword them to help you begin analytical sentences:

→ This is a strength/weakness because...

→ This similarity/difference exists because...

→ The consequence of this is...

→ This is important because...

Using these sentence starters should help you to ensure that you have moved beyond just descriptive writing. You will probably devise more of these as your writing style develops.

> ### ✓ Exam tip
>
> Remember the difference between 'analysis' and 'evaluation'. Almost all short-answer questions are looking only for analysis, so you do not need to make judgements or reason out your arguments.

Short, source-based answers (AS only)

If you are an A-level student, and sitting just the A-level exams at the end of two years, you can skip this section.

Both AQA and Edexcel have short-answer questions based on sources in the AS exams. The generic advice discussed above is still relevant for these questions, but you must also know how to interpret sources, and then integrate them into your answer. Both exam boards also award some AO3 marks for these questions, so you must also use evaluative skills.

Types of source

There are two types of source that you are most likely to encounter in a politics exam — text-based and data-based sources. While there are a myriad of political cartoons produced every day, the nature of AS questions means that you are unlikely to encounter one in your exam.

Text sources

Text sources are usually a couple of paragraphs of text, taken or adapted from a book, article or report. These will often advance one particular argument and use some evidence to support their view. Before you begin to write your answer regarding such a source, you must take the time to read it thoroughly and identify the following:

→ What is the overall viewpoint of the source?
→ What are the individual arguments in the source?
→ What evidence is used to support the arguments in the source?
→ What is the provenance of the source?

This looks like a lot of questions, but most of them you will deal with naturally when reading the source.

Understanding provenance is important in evaluating sources. In short, 'provenance' means where a source comes from. Initially, you should identify the author of the source, and where and when it was published. Once you have this information, you must consider whether this affects the meaning of the source. For example, if the source is taken from a right-wing newspaper, might that explain why they advance a certain view?

Data sources

Data sources come in a number of different formats. They may be tables of statistical data, or data which have been graphically represented, such as a pie chart or a graph. Before you begin writing your answer regarding such sources, you must take the time to identify the following:

→ What trends are there in the data (and can you explain these)?
→ Are there any anomalies in the data (and can you explain these)?
→ What do the data suggest?
→ What is the provenance of the source?

Using sources

How you use the source in your writing will vary depending on the question. However, a good rule of thumb is to expect to take most of your knowledge (AO1) from the source itself. Your job is to explain, analyse and evaluate this knowledge, or to compare it to the information you have taken from another source.

Single source questions

In the Edexcel AS exams, you will face a 10-mark question which asks you to 'explain', and all the available marks are awarded for AO1 knowledge and understanding. You should still be aiming for three paragraphs in your answer, but your focus should be on explanation and example, rather than on application.

From your source, identify three points that need explaining. This is the knowledge aspect of AO1. For each of these points, explain what it means and give supporting examples in context. This is the understanding part of AO1.

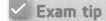
Exam tip

Have a highlighter handy in your exam, preferably two of different colours. Quickly highlight the arguments and evidence within a source, ideally in two different colours.

! Common pitfall

Bias is a terrible word. Too many students assume a 'biased' source is of little value — this could not be further from the truth. Almost all text sources advance a particular view and lay out evidence to support their view. As a student of politics, this can be useful as it will show one side of an argument, and will allow you to evaluate how strong an argument is by reviewing the evidence presented.

! Common pitfall

You need to leave yourself time to read the source. When you work out how much time you have for each question in an exam, remember this must include time to read and understand the source.

Annotated example 3.7

The annotations on Figure 3.2 show how you might answer the four questions on data sources.

Trends: Conservative membership has steadily decreased, Labour membership has increased since 2010, Liberal Democrat membership has remained stable, and third party membership has increased but is still low. *Explanation:* Labour's rise could be a reaction to the austerity policies of 2010 onwards. Third parties are still disadvantaged by FPTP and this may explain their membership figures.

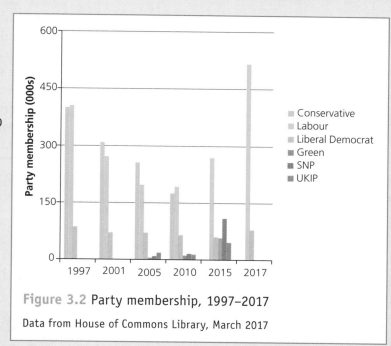

Figure 3.2 Party membership, 1997–2017

Data from House of Commons Library, March 2017

Anomalies: the figures are missing for many parties in 2017. Labour's membership had a huge jump in 2017, the SNP's membership jumped in 2015. *Explanation:* Labour's big jump may be attributed to the two leadership elections won by Corbyn, and the SNP's jump may be a reaction to the Scottish independence referendum of 2014.

Suggests: a general decline in party membership between 1997 and 2017. *Explanation:* a growth in apathy towards traditional party politics and the development of pressure groups through the internet and social media.

Provenance: this source is from the House of Common Library. *Explanation:* the House of Common Library provides impartial research and is therefore a reliable source.

Comparative source questions

In the AQA AS exams, you will face a 12-mark question with two sources. You will have to 'analyse, evaluate and compare' these sources. In the Edexcel AS exams, you will face a 10-mark question with two sources. You will be asked to 'assess' a given statement. In both cases, you should still be aiming for three paragraphs in your answer, but the structure of each paragraph will look quite different to that for single source questions. The key difference is that you must draw your points from the sources, and it is these points that you will analyse and evaluate.

To gain AO2 analysis marks in your writing, you should do two things:

→ Find a point identified in the source(s) that is relevant to your question and analyse what this means.

→ Look for similarities and differences between the sources and try to explain why these may exist.

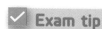 **Exam tip**

Most exam boards do not credit points if they have not been drawn from the source. To make sure that all of your points are taken from the source, you could use a short quote integrated into your first sentence.

Analysis is the same whether it is of a source or of a point made from your own knowledge. (For more information on analysis, see the advice given earlier in this chapter.)

To gain AO3 evaluation marks in your writing, you should consider two things:

→ Which of the arguments in the source(s) are stronger or weaker, and why?
→ Does the provenance of the source make it more or less reliable?

Figure 3.3 shows how the P-E-A structure can be adapted for use in a comparative source question. Use this as a guide for the rough proportions that each of these skills will take up in a handwritten paragraph.

> **! Common pitfall**
>
> Notice the change of colours here. Compared to a short-answer question, the explanation is shorter, analysis forms the bulk of the middle section, and the final section is now evaluation. Short-answer questions and short source questions have different paragraph structures.

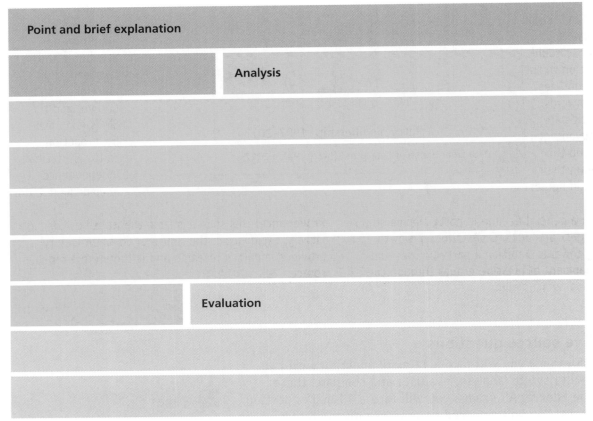

Point and brief explanation

Analysis

Evaluation

Figure 3.3 Guide to the P-E-A structure in a comparative source question

The bottom line

> Always deconstruct any question and read any source before beginning to write your answer.
> Short-answer questions do not need introductions or conclusions, and will probably include three paragraphs.
> The P-E-A rule is a good rule when writing your first politics essays, but you should use this to develop your own style as you go on.
> Evidence and examples should include some detail and should add to your paragraph, not simply repeat a theoretical point.
> Remember the key questions to ask yourself to ensure that you are being analytical.
> *AS only:* make sure you analyse and evaluate the sources in short-answer questions.

4 Writing an essay

Learning outcomes

> Be able to deconstruct any exam question so that you know exactly what it is asking
> Understand how to write effective and useful introductions and conclusions
> Know how to structure a basic essay paragraph
> Be able to maintain a line of argument throughout an essay
> Know how to be analytical and evaluative throughout an essay
> Understand how to use evidence effectively in your work
> Understand how to use sources in essays

Let's begin with a reminder: writing is a highly personal skill — it is important that you understand that there is no right way to write. So this chapter will look at some general rules and advice for essays but you will always need to integrate this into your own natural style. However, it is useful to keep this piece of advice in mind regarding essay writing: **there is no shortcut!**

Practice makes perfect and is the simplest way to improve your work. If you have chosen subjects that involve essay writing, this is hopefully because you like writing. If you can enjoy writing, rather than it being a chore, or just a way for you to get a grade, your work will improve quickly.

The difference between...

Short answers	Essays
• Short answers focus on the AO1 and AO2 skills of knowledge and understanding, and analysis.	• Essays focus on all three assessment objectives, the AO1, AO2 and AO3 skills of knowledge and understanding, analysis, and evaluation.
• They do not need introductions or conclusions.	• They need to be properly structured and include an introduction and a conclusion.
• They are more factual in their nature.	• They are more argumentative and persuasive in their nature.

In a nutshell... essays are not simply short answers with more paragraphs!

Your exam board
AQA

Table 4.1 shows how the marks are allocated in AQA essay questions.

Table 4.1 Mark scheme for AQA essay questions

Level	Marks	Command word	AO marks
AS	25	Analyse and evaluate	AO1: 7 AO2: 10 AO3: 8
A-level	25 (source)	Analyse, evaluate and compare	AO1: 5 AO2: 10 AO3: 10
A-level	25 (non-source)	Analyse and evaluate	AO1: 5 AO2: 10 AO3: 10

Edexcel

Table 4.2 shows how the marks are allocated in Edexcel essay questions.

Table 4.2 Mark scheme for Edexcel essay questions

Level	Marks	Command word	AO marks
AS	30	How far	AO1: 10 AO2: 10 AO3: 10
A-level	24	Examine	AO1: 8 AO2: 8 AO3: 8
A-level	30	Evaluate	AO1: 10 AO2: 10 AO3: 10

WJEC

Remember, WJEC has slightly different assessment objectives to AQA and Edexcel:

→ AO1: knowledge and understanding
→ AO2: interpret and apply political information to identify and explain relevant similarities, differences and connections
→ AO3: analyse and evaluate

Table 4.3 Mark scheme for WJEC essay questions

Paper	Marks	Command word	AO marks
Papers 1 and 2	22	Varies	AO1: 10 AO3: 12
Papers 3 and 4	24	Varies	AO1: 8 AO2: 16
Papers 3 and 4	40	Varies	AO1: 12 AO2: 14 AO3: 14

Deconstructing the question

Understanding what a question is asking is obviously crucial to being able to answer it effectively. Yet, as with short-answer questions, too many students skim-read the question and begin writing their answer without even pausing. It may sound obvious, but you are not being tested on what you know; you are being tested on your ability to use what you know to answer a specific question. It is crucial to understand that knowing 'stuff' is not enough for good marks at this level of study. You must be able to identify between answering the question set and simply writing everything that you know.

> **! Common pitfall**
>
> Students often have well-rehearsed essays that they are comfortable with, and when a similar question comes up in an exam, they simply regurgitate this. If you do not answer the exact question asked, you are unlikely to achieve as highly as you could.

The difference between...

Evaluate the view that the US Constitution is increasingly out of date.

(30 marks)

Answering the question set	Regurgitating everything you know
The Second Amendment is out of date as the USA has the world's largest military.	Checks and balances create gridlock which means the Constitution is weak.
The vague nature of the Constitution has allowed for interpretive amendments, which has kept it up to date.	The codification of the US Constitution protects the powers of each branch, making it strong.
Expert comment: the information here explicitly focuses on change, or lack of change, over time, which is exactly what the question is asking for.	*Expert comment: in this example, the information is accurate but irrelevant — the question is not about the strengths and weaknesses of the Constitution.*

To deconstruct essay questions, you will need to build on the deconstruction skills discussed in Chapter 3. You can do this by taking the C-F-L approach:

C — command word(s)

F — focus

L — limitation

> **✓ Exam tip**
>
> The C-F-L approach can usefully be applied to short-answer questions too, but is a must for essay questions to ensure you are actually answering the question set, not the question that you hoped would come up.

> **✓ Exam tip**
>
> There is no 'one' expected answer to any essay and understanding this is crucial to being a good student. Every student will analyse it differently, and refer to different points. You must have your own opinion about a question and justify each point.

> **! Common pitfall**
>
> If you do not care about what you have studied, it is difficult to write persuasively about it. Even if only for the duration of the exam, you must find some passion for politics if your writing is to be persuasive.

Command words

The command word is the word that tells you what to do. In an essay question, these are most commonly 'analyse', 'evaluate', 'to what extent' and 'how far'. But you must also be aware that essay questions normally cover all three AOs, meaning you will also have to deploy knowledge, analyse it and evaluate it.

Table 4.4 Common command words in essay questions

Command word	AO it is linked to	What you need to do
Analyse and evaluate	AO1, AO2, AO3	Break down each point or argument into parts and show how it works before making a reasoned judgement on the significance or not of each point or argument.
Discuss	AO1, AO2, AO3	Usually, you are asked to discuss a given statement. You are effectively writing a debate about the statement, analysing reasons why it could be considered accurate or not, and making a reasoned judgement on these reasons.
Evaluate	AO1, AO2, AO3	Reach a judgement as to how far you agree or disagree with a given statement or view by analysing a range of factors on both sides of the argument and evaluating their significance and/or strength before reaching a well-justified conclusion.
How far To what extent	AO1, AO2, AO3	These commands are very similar. It is best to imagine that these questions are asking you to judge something on a sliding scale: Not at all — Somewhat — A lot — Completely To achieve this, you need to analyse and evaluate all the evidence from a range of views, before making your own judgement as to where on this line the answer should be.

Focus

The 'focus' of a question can include a number of words or phrases within a question, but in short it is the **topic(s)** of the question and the **debate** that you are being asked about.

The topic(s) should be something you have studied and (hopefully) revised. It could be a broad topic, for example 'Parliament', which encompasses both the House of Commons and the House of Lords, or it might be more specific, for example 'backbenchers', which is only those MPs in the House of Commons who do not hold government positions.

The debate is the words or phrase within a question that tells you what argument you should be writing about. This is usually a more conceptual or theoretical phrase, such as 'power', 'influence', 'reform' and so on.

Being clear on both of these will help to ensure that everything you write is tightly focused on the exact question you have been asked.

! **Common pitfall**

'How far' and 'to what extent' questions are not 'yes' or 'no' questions. You have been asked to judge the level of agreement with a statement, and you should explain how you reached this judgement.

Activity

Can you identify the focus of these questions?

- Evaluate the extent to which the prime minister can control their cabinet.   (30 marks, Edexcel)
- 'Further constitutional reform in the UK is necessary.' Analyse and evaluate this statement.   (25 marks, AQA)

Limitation

Not all questions have limitations, but you need to be aware of them just in case they do. A limitation is a phrase or word within the question that restricts what you can talk about in your answer. This may be an obvious limitation that restricts the individuals or time period you can discuss. If a question asks about 'the Coalition' or includes the phrase 'since 1997', then writing about other governments or examples from before 1997 will be worth few, if any, marks. In this sense, the difference between the focus of a question and its limitation is often minimal.

More tricky to spot are the small, often unnoticed, words that give context to the question. These are phrases like 'increasingly', 'now' or 'become'. All of these phrases suggest that a change over time has taken place which has made the debate more or less important. To gain top marks, recognising this is crucial as it may change a relatively simple 'strengths and weaknesses' debate into something more complex that requires explicit analysis of political circumstances.

Not all questions will have clear limitations. Once you understand what you are looking for, you should be able to quickly identify limitations in a question — do not spend ages looking for one if it is not there.

The difference between...

A question with a limitation	A question without a limitation
'Reform of first-past-the-post has become a necessity.' Analyse and evaluate this statement. (25 marks)	**Evaluate the view that a proportional electoral system should be used for UK general elections. (30 marks)**
The limitation 'has become' means some of the arguments surrounding electoral reform are less valid in this essay. For example, to say that first-past-the-post creates wasted votes is not a new phenomenon; this has not 'become' a problem, it has always been a problem.	The lack of limitations in this question means that a discussion of wasted votes would be more valid, as proportional systems would reduce the number of wasted votes.

Despite the high degree of similarity in the two questions above, the same point is not equally valid because of the limitation.

Annotated example 4.1

The topic focus is the House of Lords.

'The House of Lords is now an effective check on the power of the government in the UK.' Analyse and evaluate this statement. (25 marks)

The command words.

The limitation is 'now'.

The debate is the effectiveness of House of Lords' power to check government.

In this example, the focus is only on the House of Lords, so anything on the House of Commons is irrelevant. Equally, the focus is only on its role in checking the power of the UK government, so anything written about its representative role, for example, is of no value. Finally, 'now' is a limitation as this suggests that something has changed recently which has made them more effective — it is your job to show what. If you write a bland essay about the strengths and weakness of the House of Lords, you will not have answered the question.

Activities

- Get the specification for your exams and use it to try and create your own questions. This is also a brilliant way to revise.
- Find some past paper questions and, using the C-F-L approach and your own knowledge, try to rewrite the questions into simpler language. Be careful not to twist or change the question, however.

Planning your essay

Now you know what the question is asking of you, it is important to take some time to plan your essay.

If you are planning an essay that you are completing at home, your plan should take up no more than one side of A4 paper. This will make it easier to use once you do begin writing. A good plan will cover:

→ what will be in your introduction

→ each point you plan to cover, including examples

→ what conclusion you plan to reach

> **! Common pitfall**
>
> Whether it is for homework or in the exam, too many students do not plan their work. Planning homework and planning an exam essay are different skills, but you should always plan your essays. It will avoid you wandering off on a tangent as you write.
> (For more on how to plan an essay in timed conditions, see Chapter 5.)

Annotated example 4.2

Evaluate the extent to which the prime minister can control their cabinet.   (30 marks)

A good plan may look like the following.

Structure	Topic	Detail
Introduction	Define	Cabinet
	Discuss	PM can hire/fire But PM must be wary as cabinet can unseat them
	Direction	Can control but level of control depends on circumstances
Point 1	Hire/fire	✓ PM hires favourites, e.g. May reshuffle in 2017 and Gove ✗ Big beasts usually need to be in cabinet, e.g. Johnson Link big beasts to collective responsibility
Point 2	Collective ministerial responsibility (CMR)	✓ CMR means PM is protected from criticism, e.g. Brexit ✗ Cannot stop ministers resigning which can be damaging, e.g. Cook/Short Link CMR to controls agenda Link resigning to unseating PM
Point 3	Control agenda	✓ PM makes cabinet committees, e.g. Blair ✗ Media/large depts./circumstances can dictate agenda, e.g terrorism/COBRA
Point 4	Cabinet can unseat PM	✓ PM can effectively be forced out, e.g. Thatcher ✗ Very rare (but due to rare circumstances or wariness of cabinet?)
Conclusion		Control over cabinet logistics and personal power of PM make cabinet more dependent on PM than vice versa. PM predominantly controls cabinet; rare circumstances are just that, rare.

Certainly, it is vital that you know what conclusion you plan to reach before writing. Knowing this will help you drop hints throughout your essay so that by the time your examiner gets to the conclusion, they already know what you are going to conclude.

In example 4.2, the student has highlighted various ways in which the same point can be interpreted, and has identified the examples they plan to use and the conclusion they want to reach.

Having written your plan, you can have it on your desk when you are writing your essay to ensure that you remain focused on the question and use the best examples you can to illustrate each point.

Writing introductions

One of the most common mistakes that students make when essay writing is spending valuable time on an introduction that ultimately gains few, or often no, marks. Most students are aware they should write an introduction, but are rarely taught how to do so; even more rarely are they taught how to do so effectively. Yet, if you follow some simple advice it is remarkably easy to write a worthwhile introduction.

Why should I write an introduction?

Unless you know the reason why you are writing an introduction, writing one is rather pointless. Sadly, the most common answer students give to this question is 'to introduce their essay'. Even worse is when introductions are nothing more than the question simply rephrased.

! Common pitfall

Your plan should not include absolutely everything. In fact, usually it will include more AO1 knowledge than anything else. Ensure that you are only using your plan to guide you. You still need to add in your analysis and evaluation as you go.

✓ Exam tip

If you have planned an essay for homework, still try and complete the essay itself in timed conditions. This is great practice for the exam.

The difference between...

Evaluate the extent to which the prime minister can control their cabinet.
(30 marks)

A good introduction	A poor introduction
As the head of the executive branch, the prime minister (PM) retains the power to hire to and fire from their cabinet as he sees fit. Traditionally, the role of 'primus inter pares' has been nothing more than theoretical, with the PM using such power to dominate the direction and power of their cabinet. Nonetheless, this power is not unlimited, and in times of small majorities, low poll ratings and unforeseen national crises, the PM's domination is increasingly challenged and difficult to maintain. Certainly, the trend in recent years for small electoral wins, coupled with factions within parties that need controlling, has meant that despite the PM's power remaining notable, the cabinet has been resurgent.	There are a number of ways in which a prime minister (PM) can dominate their cabinet. However, there are also ways in which the cabinet can have power over the PM. It depends on a number of factors where this power lies.
Expert comment:	Expert comment:
• The introduction, and the conclusion, should each take up about 1/10th of your essay.	• This introduction is too short and simply repeats the question.
• This introduction shows an understanding of the key terms, 'prime minister', 'cabinet' and 'control'.	• There is no evidence of understanding of what the question is asking.
• It identifies various arguments that will be discussed — hiring and firing, majorities, and so on.	• There is no suggestion of the topics the student will be discussing in their essay.
• There is a clear line of argument throughout, hinting which way the student will argue.	• There is no suggestion of which way the student plans to argue throughout their essay.

Annotated example 4.3

To what extent do anarchists agree over the role of human nature? (24 marks)

> To some extent, anarchists do share common views about human nature. However, there are some divisions between anarchists where they do disagree. This essay will evaluate the extent of their agreement.

This is a poor introduction which would gain no marks. It is little more than the question rephrased.

Introductions like the one in example 4.3 tell the examiner one thing only — that you plan on attempting the question. Given that you turned up to the exam, or that you actually did your homework, then we can assume they already knew that. Equally, this introduction suggests there are two sides to the answer, but again your examiner and teacher already knew that, and you have not shown you know what these two sides are.

You should write an introduction for a number of reasons:

→ It should show the examiner that you know what specifically the question is asking of you.
→ It should highlight that you have some relevant knowledge.
→ It should act as a minimal 'contents page' for your essay so the examiner has some idea what is coming.
→ It should put the debate in context.
→ It should give a hint about the line of argument you plan to follow.

That seems like quite a lot for an introduction, but actually it can be achieved concisely. Also, while marks are not allocated for introductions alone, it suggests to the examiner that you understand how to write an essay, debate and argue — all before they have even read one of your proper paragraphs.

How do I write an effective introduction?

An effective introduction can be achieved in three simple steps or the **'three Ds': define, discuss, direction**.

Define

The opening line of an introduction can be as simple as defining the key terms within a question, but you do need to exercise some judgement here. There are certain common terms that do not need defining — these tend to be institutions. For example, there is no need to define what a parliament is, or what an election is. However, if there is specific or conceptual terminology, defining these demonstrates your knowledge and also helps to keep you focused on the question. For example, if a question includes phrases like 'sovereignty', 'imperial presidency' or 'first-past-the-post', you might spend just a sentence outlining what these mean.

> ✓ **Exam tip**
>
> The 'define' part of an introduction should be contained in one sentence.

Annotated example 4.4

Evaluate the extent to which the prime minister can control their cabinet.   (30 marks)

> The cabinet in the UK consists of senior government ministers, appointed by the prime minister, who develop and direct government policy.

This sentence defines the relationship between the prime minister and cabinet which is suggested in the question and even highlights one method of control.

If there is no term that needs defining in a question, you might instead choose to define the context of the question.

Annotated example 4.5

'Further constitutional reform in the UK is necessary.' Analyse and evaluate this statement. (25 marks)

> Since 1997, the UK constitution has undergone extensive reform with the creation of the UK Supreme Court and devolution to Scotland and Wales among many other reforms.

This sentence effectively helps to define the word 'further' in the question, placing the debate in context and demonstrating specific knowledge to your examiner.

Discuss

The discussion step should make up the bulk of your introduction. In the time-pressured circumstances of an exam, this means it is likely to be between two and four sentences. You should aim to outline the sides of the debate you plan to discuss, and even consider dropping in the name of an example you plan to discuss. This is the part of your introduction that is effectively the contents page for your essay, and what you choose to put in here should be the arguments that you believe to be the most significant with regard to the question set.

Annotated example 4.6

'Further constitutional reform in the UK is necessary.' Analyse and evaluate this statement.

(25 marks)

This shows the student has good, up-to-date knowledge of the political context.

This begins to hint at the view of the student, which hopefully they will justify later on.

The student has identified more points they plan to discuss in their essay.

> Following the hung parliament of 2017, the case for electoral reform has never been more pressing. Nonetheless, reformed aspects of the constitution such as the House of Lords and devolution seem to be functioning well and with limited public opposition. Indeed, in recent referendums, the public have rejected further reform.

The student highlights one of the points they plan to discuss.

As the question is about 'further reform', it suggests some reform has already happened. The student has not simply named it (which would be irrelevant to this question), they imply that as reform is working well, further reform is not necessary.

From this example, you can see that in just three sentences, this student has shown the examiner they have good knowledge of political theory in context, and has demonstrated what they plan to discuss by dropping in a few examples.

Direction

The direction step is where you can begin to hint to the examiner the likely outcome of your essay. Your essays are a work of persuasion — you are not supposed to be simply describing everything you have learnt; you are supposed to persuade the reader that your answer to the question set is correct. This should be woven throughout your whole essay, starting with the introduction.

The direction should be no more than a sentence, which hints at what you plan to argue and why. As this is an introduction, and you have not yet presented your argument, you must be careful not to conclude. Instead, use phrases that have some flexibility in them such as 'it seems', 'it appears' or 'it may be that'.

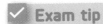 **Exam tip**

Spending time planning and ensuring you know what your line of argument is before you begin is crucial. It will prevent you getting halfway through and realising you do not agree with your own direction.

Annotated example 4.7

'Further constitutional reform in the UK is necessary.' Analyse and evaluate this statement.   (25 marks)

The student hints at their argument.

> Given the lack of political and public desire for further reform, it seems unlikely that it is in fact 'necessary'.

The student identifies a reason to justify their decision.

The student uses a word from the question to show their focus is on what they have been asked.

Activity

Find an essay you have already completed. Using the three Ds, try and improve on your introduction. Ask your teacher to review it with you.

Writing an analytical and evaluative essay

With the introduction out of the way, you can now look to writing the main bulk of your essay. Unlike short-answer questions, your writing needs to be far more discursive and persuasive. Students who stick rigidly to a clinical formula will often produce work that lacks passion and persuasion.

Writing paragraphs

While the P-E-A approach you learnt about in Chapter 3 makes for a good foundation for writing paragraphs in essays, it does not go far enough, nor does it achieve all of the assessment objectives. Therefore, this structure needs to be developed.

First, you need to identify the points that you plan to discuss.

> **! Common pitfall**
>
> Do not change your line of argument halfway through your answer. If your introduction and conclusion do not suggest the same answer, the result is likely to be a poorly argued essay.

Annotated example 4.8

Evaluate the view that backbenchers are effectively powerless.

(30 marks)

> Points I plan to make:
>
> ● backbench rebellions
>
> ● role on select committees
>
> ● asking questions at PMQs
>
> ● urgent questions

However, for each of these points, it could be argued that they show **both** backbenchers' power **and** their lack of power. For example, backbench rebellions can be:

● powerful — they have been successful, such as preventing military action in Syria in 2013.
● weak — they are rare even on controversial legislation, e.g. the Brexit bill passed by over 300 votes in 2017.

As there are clearly two ways in which the same point can be analysed, simply applying the P-E-A approach in this level of essay will only gain you some marks. Instead, your paragraph needs to be more complex. You will need to decide which of these interpretations you believe to be stronger. In writing one paragraph on this point, you then need to show both interpretations, but analyse and evaluate to show which one is more persuasive.

> **✓ Exam tip**
>
> Avoid using 'I', 'you' or 'we'. If you read your textbooks, you will find most do not do this. Usually, if you have written a phrase such as 'I think', this can simply be deleted from the beginning of a sentence and the sentence will still make sense. This is a far more academic way of writing.

It is important that you include **both** interpretations in your work. If you ignore one half of the argument, it suggests that you are unable to explain why one side is more persuasive than the other, or that you have not recognised that there are two sides. Either way, it makes the argument you are trying to make flawed. Instead you must show both sides, but show why you believe one to be more persuasive than the other.

Annotated example 4.9

Evaluate the view that backbenchers are effectively powerless.   (30 marks)

Backbench MPs have often been considered to be powerless due to the strength of the party whip. The whip maintains discipline within each party, expecting party loyalty from MPs when they vote. Those backbenchers who defy the whip often are unlikely to find that they can advance their career within the party, meaning that backbench rebellions are reasonably uncommon with Cameron being defeated on only nine occasions during his time as prime minister. However, nine defeats is a considerable increase and backbench rebellions have become increasingly common. Indeed, the 2010 Parliament was the most rebellious since the Second World War, suggesting that backbench power has in fact grown. Certainly in times of small majorities, backbench rebellions hold the potential to be more powerful as they can prevent the government winning a vote. Theresa May, having not won an overall majority in the 2017 election, had to abandon plans for grammar schools rather than risk such a defeat. This suggests that there are certain circumstances in which backbenchers can exercise considerable power over the government, and such power cannot simply be measured by defeats alone. While backbench power may not have been evident during times of large majorities, such as Blair experienced in 1997, the last three elections have returned either hung parliaments or small majorities. The recent trend of small majorities suggests that at least currently, backbench MPs actually retain more power than they have previously had.

| **Key:** | AO1 | AO2 | AO3 |

This longer paragraph covers both sides of the argument, supports both sides with relevant and recent evidence, but maintains the argument throughout that backbenchers do actually have some power. It also addresses why some people may say backbenchers are weak, before suggesting this view is wrong due to current political circumstances. If you do not make a judgement in your work, and of course show how you reached this judgement, you are not being evaluative. In this case, the student justifies their argument by context — they say that backbenchers have power currently due to the small majority.

The paragraph is colour-coded so that you can begin to see how AO1, AO2 and AO3 are blended together to create a single paragraph covering both interpretations of a point. While this colour-coding is a little blunt, and could be debated, it should help you begin to understand the nuances of writing a complex paragraph like this.

Activity

Find an essay that you have written and try to colour-code one paragraph from it in the way shown in example 4.9. Does your paragraph have the right balance, or do you rely more on one AO than another? Re-attempt this paragraph to improve the balance and structure.

! Common pitfalls

- Avoid rhetorical questions. It is your job to answer the questions set, not make up more.
- Students often forget that examples are AO1 — either they are knowledge or they demonstrate that you understand the context. Therefore, do not spend endless lines writing about many different examples. Using one example well within your paragraph is better than identifying many.
- Often students break one point into two paragraphs — for and against. By doing this, you are being more descriptive than analytical or evaluative, meaning you are not demonstrating the AOs effectively.

The all-important context

When writing a politics essay, it is important to recognise that you are writing about an ever-changing subject and that political circumstances may change your answer to a particular question.

Annotated example 4.10

Evaluate the view that the UK prime minister is more like a president. (30 marks)

Using knowledge that you have gained throughout your studies, you could review three recent prime ministers who may be considered strong, average and weak in terms of their power. For each one, however, this is perhaps explained by their majority.

	Blair	Cameron	May
Assessment of power	Strong	Average	Weak
Seats	418/659 (1997)	331/650 (2015)	318/650 (2017)

Blair had a huge majority in 1997.   Cameron had a small majority in 2015.   May failed to gain a majority in 2017.

This helps to explain that some prime ministers may be able to act more presidentially because of their majority, but that this may change at the next election.

To delve deeper into this, you can look at just one prime minister. For example, Thatcher is often considered to be a strong prime minister, yet she was unseated by her own cabinet — circumstances change.

To achieve the top grades, you must show an awareness of circumstances. This means you might address issues in your writing such as:

→ Has a situation changed recently?
→ Are there trends that have continued?
→ Are there different circumstances that affect your answer?
→ Why might this question be more important today?

In example 4.10, it might be that you decide that a prime minister is like a president during a time of national emergency, but more like a prime minister when it comes to deciding domestic policy. Equally, in reviewing change over time, you may decide that the development of technology has enabled prime ministers to be more presidential, but equally that it has opened them up to more criticism which may weaken their position.

Recognising the importance of political circumstance will make your arguments stronger. There will always be exceptions for every argument, but by their very nature exceptions are a rarity. If you can identify these, and identify the more common trends, you will have a much stronger foundation for your argument. You can see this in action in example 4.9 — the evaluation that recent trends have been for smaller majorities is the justification for the student's view that backbench MPs have power.

Structuring your essay

Having written one strong paragraph, it is important to understand how that fits into the overall structure of an essay. From start to finish, your essay should be persuasive — your job is not to outline all of the possible arguments but to convince the reader that you are right, based on critical and analysis and evaluation.

A good essay structure will have a basic structure of:

→ Introduction
→ Main debate
→ Conclusion

However, how you structure the main debate is important to your line of argument.

> **! Common pitfall**
>
> Students often start sentences containing an example by writing, 'For example…'. There is nothing wrong with this, but it is unnecessary. Once you start talking about names, dates and so on it becomes obvious that it is an example. Deleting this sentence starter will make your writing look more mature.

The difference between…

Evaluate the view that backbenchers are effectively powerless.   (30 marks)

Compare the structures below, arguing that backbenchers are actually powerful.

A strong persuasive structure	A weak persuasive structure
Introduction	**Introduction**
Most significant point: include for and against in one paragraph. Line of argument is for.	**Most significant point:** for.
	Most significant point: against.
Point 2: include for and against in one paragraph. Line of argument is for.	**Point 2:** for.
	Point 2: against.
Point 3: include for and against in one paragraph. Line of argument is against.	**Point 3:** for.
	Point 3: against.
Point 4: include for and against in one paragraph. Line of argument is for.	**Point 4:** for.
	Point 4: against.
Conclusion	**Conclusion**
Using this structure, the student writes fewer paragraphs but each paragraph shows both interpretations of a point and reaches a justified evaluation. They do not include any fewer negative points, but within each paragraph they show why the positive outweighs the negative. This student is likely to be more closely focused on the question, and therefore will be rewarded more highly.	Using this structure, the student produces a totally balanced essay that suggests the arguments for and against are equal. This suggests their AO2 analysis is weak and their AO3 evaluation is almost completely missing. This approach relies on telling an examiner everything you know, rather than showing why it is relevant to the question.

It is important that you do not see your essays like a sports match — you cannot evaluate which side of an argument is stronger by seeing how many paragraphs fall on either side. Instead, you must also evaluate the importance of each point that you have made. Using the 'strong persuasive structure' on page 60, the student could theoretically have only one paragraph in favour of their view, which they may consider to be so important that it outweighs all the other points. While this is unlikely, as long as you can show critical analysis and evaluation in reaching this judgement, it is still a valid approach.

Making your essay flow

While each paragraph should be on a separate point, your essay should flow naturally from one point to the next, highlighting connections. It should not read as though each paragraph is a mini-essay on its own. You can achieve these paragraph transitions through connective phrases such as:

→ While...

→ Despite this...

→ In addition...

→ It is also important to...

Additionally, you may be able to use some of the language or trends from your previous paragraph to help you open your new paragraph.

> **✓ Exam tip**
>
> Leave a line between each paragraph. It will make your work much easier to read and your arguments will be clearer.

> **! Common pitfall**
>
> Do not try and include **every** factor that might be relevant to an essay. Depth of analysis and evaluation is better than breadth, and by choosing the most important factors you will already be demonstrating judgement.

Annotated example 4.11

Evaluate the view that backbenchers are effectively powerless. (30 marks)

To follow on from the colour-coded paragraph in example 4.9, you might open the next paragraph like this:

This is clearly a link from the previous paragraph.

> The recent trend for smaller majorities has also allowed backbenchers to exert power through urgent questions.

The point you are moving on to is clearly identified.

Such a transition is important as it helps your essays to read as one persuasive piece of text and is a more mature way of making an argument.

Take it further

The *Study Skills Handbook* by Stella Cottrell offers advice on other connective phrases that you could utilise in your essays.

Writing conclusions

Conclusions are often a huge annoyance for students — they often do not know how to do them or run out of time in the exam to complete them properly. Unfortunately, for too many students, their conclusion is just one sentence — and this is not enough at all. The conclusion is crucial for top marks as it is your chance to answer the whole question rather than the individual factors that make up a question. If you read any of the exam questions, they are all asking you to make a judgement:

→ *Evaluate* the *extent* to which the prime minister can control their cabinet. (30 marks)

→ 'Further constitutional reform in the UK is *necessary*.' *Analyse* and *evaluate* this statement. (25 marks)

→ *To what extent* do anarchists *agree* over the role of human nature? (24 marks)

The answers to these questions are not simply 'yes' or 'no'. In your essay you might have dealt with specific factors relating to the question, but now you are at the end you need to stand back from these details and make a decision overall. A conclusion should be the direct answer to the question, with a justification of how you reached your decision. It should put together the overall themes of your essay to reach a final judgement, as shown in Figure 4.1.

Throughout your essay, you will have broken down the question into a number of factors and judged each one individually. Your conclusion should aim to reassemble these points so that you can reach one overall judgement. In this sense, it is a bit like the verdict in a court trial, as shown in Figure 4.2.

In this analogy, the jury has to reach a verdict of guilty or not guilty based on all of the evidence, not just some of it. This is the same as your conclusion — it should be an overall view, not simply restating each one of your paragraphs.

> ## ✓ Exam tip
>
> The answer to almost all essays is, 'it depends on the circumstances'. It is your job to justify what those circumstances are and when they are more or less significant. A president's power may vary depending on how close to the election he is, for example.

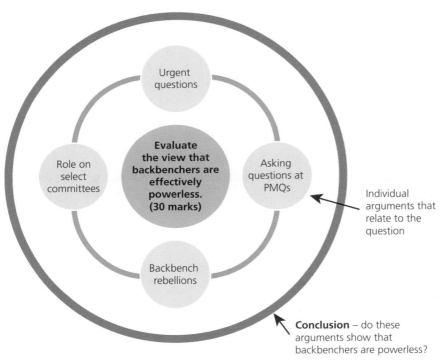

Figure 4.1 Concluding your essay

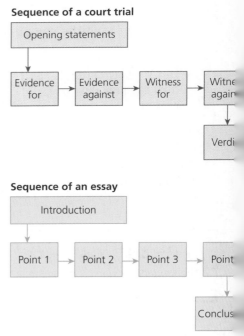

Figure 4.2 The sequence of a court trial and an essay

Annotated example 4.12

Evaluate the view that backbenchers are effectively powerless.

(30 marks)

A clear and concise judgement, directly answering the question.

Again, an implied link to a paragraph, without repeating it. By drawing this and 'political circumstances' together, the student has identified a theme of change.

The student has drawn a thematic distinction. This is helpful as it justifies the type of power they believe MPs have gained.

A succinct, final judgement that uses a quote from the question to ensure they have directly answered it.

> While backbench power is not unlimited, it is clear that they have undergone an extensive growth of their power, driven by the political circumstances of the last decade and the Wright Committee reforms to the House of Commons. This has allowed backbench MPs to gain greater freedom from their party, which has allowed them to exert power upon the government without fear of reprisals which may end their career. Additionally, while the roles that they do have may not have direct power, the development of technology has meant that backbench MPs have greater opportunities for indirect power through the media. It remains unclear whether they will retain such power if a government gains a large majority, but currently, backbench MPs are certainly not 'powerless'.

The student is showing they are not ignorant of the two-sided nature of the debate.

The student has not gone into detail repeating their points, they have just highlighted the link they want to make, in this case referencing the small majorities of recent governments.

This whole sentence justifies why, overall, the student believes backbenchers are more powerful. In this case, it is the theme that they have gained freedom from party control.

Writing conclusions is a tricky skill to master, but it is crucial for AO3 marks. Table 4.5 lists a number of simple dos and don'ts that will help you develop your conclusion-writing skills.

Table 4.5 Dos and don'ts when writing a conclusion

Do	Don't
• Try to identify common themes between the points that you have made. • Make a clear decision. • Justify why you have reached that decision. • Use words from the question. • Use the word 'because' to ensure that you have tried to justify your answer. For example, 'It is clear backbenchers are not powerless because…'	• Introduce new evidence or ideas. • Always start with 'In conclusion…' or 'Therefore…' • Repeat each one of your paragraphs in turn. • Simply ignore the alternative view. It should be clear by the conclusion why your view is 'right' but do not be too rigid.

Developing your writing skills

Feedback and reflection

Once you have written an essay and had some feedback from your teacher, you should start to think about how you can develop your writing to improve it. Reflecting on your work is crucial to success at A-level.

The most important way in which you can develop your writing skills is to read the feedback that you have received from your teacher. Everybody writes differently, so once you have acted upon the generic advice in this book, your teacher will be able to give you specific advice about your own writing. However, you must do more than simply read your feedback, you must act upon it.

After each piece of written work, try to reflect on it by completing Table 4.6.

Table 4.6 Reflection and target-setting

Title:	Mark:
One thing that I did well:	
Two things that I can improve:	

Activity

Turn to Appendix 2 for some blank reflection sheets to complete after each essay that you do. The more honest, frequent and reflective you are, the more quickly your writing will improve.

The 'thing you did well' should be something that you aim to repeat in a future essay and is personal to you. This might be that your introduction was excellent, or that you had a clear line of argument, or that you stuck to the appropriate length by being more concise. Do not simply rely on self-congratulatory statements like, 'I got a good mark'. While this might make you feel good, it will not help you repeat your success.

Take it further

Spend some time looking through Manchester University's Academic Phrasebank for some ideas on connectives and sentence stems that you can integrate into your work: www.phrasebank.manchester.ac.uk/

For 'two things that I can improve', you must try to pick the two most important and specific things that you will target in your next piece. Your teacher may offer some suggestions or you may have some of your own, such as 'reducing the length of my introduction', or 'including more detail in my examples to analyse their relevance'. You should not pick more than two things — writing is a skill that improves through practice, and trying to improve everything all at once is unlikely to be effective.

You should also consider re-attempting your work, or sections of your work, heeding the feedback you have been given. It may be that you only re-attempt the introduction, conclusion, or just one paragraph, rather than the whole thing. Applying feedback in this way is a really effective way of seeing your writing develop, and you can compare your first and second attempts to see just how far you have come.

Once you have completed your reflection, you need to keep it somewhere safe and get it out for review before you try your next

! Common pitfall

Too many students focus only on the grade they receive. This is a two-year course — some of your early grades might not be A grades… yet.
Instead, try to ignore the grades, and focus instead on what has been written to work towards those A grades.

✓ Exam tip

Read your essays out loud. It is remarkable how many errors or misunderstandings you might find when you hear your work aloud. This is a great proofreading tip.

! Common pitfall

Reflection is a great exercise but if you find you are setting the same things for improvement after every essay, then you are not applying your feedback. For feedback to be effective, you must reflect on your work and act upon it.

essay. There is no point filing it away never to be seen again. Feedback is the single most important way that you can improve your writing.

Using your peers

It is easy as a student to get totally focused on your own work and feedback on your work. But, if everyone in your class has completed the same essay, then there is a wealth of opportunity for you to see how other people have written and interpreted the same information as you. Could you:

→ Ask someone in your class if you can read their essay?

→ Ask a classmate to proofread your essay and offer suggestions?

→ Colour-code a paragraph in a classmate's essay to see how they structure a paragraph?

→ Try to rewrite a classmate's paragraph to improve it?

These activities are really useful as you will see work written by people at the same level as you. You might learn new connectives or sentence stems that you can use, or find a way of interpreting evidence or structuring a paragraph that you had not thought of.

You can develop this further using technology. You might be able to use Google Docs or another collaborative piece of software to enable you all to edit one document to try and create a 'perfect' essay.

> ### Activity
>
> Pick an essay question and, with a peer, try planning your answer together to create one plan. Then write your answers separately. Compare the differences in the two essays written from this identical plan, and see if you can learn some new skills.

Essay-writing competitions

Another way you can develop your writing skills is to enter essay-writing competitions. There are lots of these, usually run by universities or similar organisations, and they will give you an opportunity to research and write on a topic in an undergraduate style. These competitions will expect well-written work, including footnotes and bibliographies to demonstrate your use of research.

> ### Take it further
>
> A brief search on Google for 'how to footnote', 'how to reference' or 'how to create a bibliography' will yield lots of advice from universities. Choose a university you might consider applying to and look at their advice on these topics.

Some of the essay competitions available for politics, or that have politics-related questions, include:

→ **R.A. Butler Politics Prize** — an essay competition by Trinity College, Cambridge with a choice of ten questions: www.trin.cam.ac.uk/undergraduate/essay-prizes/

> ### ! Common pitfall
>
> It can be easy to forget, but you are not competing against your peers. Ultimately, your goal should be to impress the examiner, and if your peers can help you do that then let them. So, work together.

> ### ! Common pitfall
>
> Be wary of plagiarism. Plagiarism is taking someone else's work and claiming it is your own. This might be as obvious as copy-and-pasting, but even if you rewrite someone else's research in your own words, you are still plagiarising. Instead, you must reference where you have used someone else's work in your own.

→ **History of Parliament Competition** — an essay competition in which you can write on any topic of your choosing relating to parliamentary or political history:
www.historyofparliamentonline.org/schools

→ **Robson History Prize** — an history-based essay competition from Trinity College, Cambridge. There is choice of around 90 questions, many of which are politically themed:
www.trin.cam.ac.uk/undergraduate/essay-prizes/

→ **John Locke Institute Essay Competition** — an essay competition with titles on politics, history, philosophy, law and economics to choose from:
www.johnlockeinstitute.com

→ **The Orwell Youth Prize** — a writing competition that encourages entries in differing styles of writing (not just essays) on political themes:
www.orwellfoundation.com/the-orwell-youth-prize/

There are others that emerge annually, and you can search on Google for these. While they often have monetary prizes, more importantly they will challenge you to develop your own writing and be a valuable addition to your university application too.

Source questions

You will be faced with a 25-mark (AQA) or 30-mark (Edexcel) question which asks you to analyse and evaluate arguments from a source, in an essay format. All of the advice above applies to this type of question too, but there are some differences.

As the source is a text source, the first thing you need to do is identify all of the arguments within the source. You can do this quickly by taking a highlighter and just identifying all of the arguments.

Annotated example 4.13

First-past-the-post — a case for reform?

The 2017 election demonstrated once again that first-past-the-post (FPTP) is long due for reform. The traditional argument that this electoral system provides a strong and stable government has once again been undermined. In only two of the last three elections has the government been formed from a single party with an outright majority. As a result, not only is the legitimacy of the government in question, Theresa May has been forced to back away from some of the electoral promises made in her campaign.

An argument about strong and stable governments

An argument about the traditionally majoritarian nature of FPTP

An argument about voter value

An argument about the 'one person, one vote' principle

An argument about tactical voting

An argument about safe seats and electoral deserts

> Equally, third parties have remained disadvantaged. While the UKIP vote predictably collapsed, the average number of votes each party needed to gain a seat varied wildly — the Liberal Democrats needed 197,659 per seat compared to just 27,930 for each SNP seat. The continued problem of wasted votes that this compounds is simply not in keeping with the principles of a liberal democracy.
>
> While voter turnout increased once again, this was more likely to do with the heavily Brexit-based campaign rather than a broader increase in political engagement. Public dissatisfaction with FPTP was evident from the growth of vote-swapping websites in order to overcome geographical inaccuracies of the system.

Once you have done this, your essay should be written and planned in much the same way as any other essay. However, you must ensure that each point that you discuss is drawn directly from the source. You need to use your own knowledge to explain what the point means, analyse it and evaluate it, but you will not be rewarded for writing about points which are not in the source.

The question will also ask you to 'compare' arguments. To do this, you may make reference to how the arguments are linked, or to one argument being stronger than another. In example 4.13, you might show a link between wasted votes and tactical voting. Equally, you might judge that undermining liberal democracy is far more concerning than the argument about a lack of 'strong and stable' governments, as the latter is only a recent phenomenon.

Just like a normal essay, you need a conclusion for this type of question. In addition, to gain AO3 marks, you must evaluate the strengths and weaknesses of the arguments. You may choose to include in your conclusion some judgement on the overall strength or weakness of the source. This would be a natural place to include comments on the provenance of the source if you have not done so already in your essay.

For more advice on dealing with sources, see Chapter 3.

The bottom line

> Deconstructing a question using the C-F-L approach will help you to keep focused on exactly what the question is asking.

> Planning your essays is important and you should have begun to develop an effective way to do this when time is not an issue.

> An effective and useful introduction can be written using the 'three Ds' method.

> Your line of argument should be woven throughout the structure of your essay, and its paragraphs.

> An effective conclusion focuses on the broad themes of your essay, not the individual points.

> Using feedback, reflection, re-attempting work and practising in timed conditions is key to developing your own work.

> *AQA only* — when writing an essay about a source, all points must be drawn from the source.

5

Exam skills

Learning outcomes

> Knowing how to plan and structure your essay in exam conditions
> Being able to pick the right question quickly
> Managing your time in an exam
> Developing effective revision strategies

Lots of the advice so far will help you to develop the skills necessary to succeed in politics. However, when it comes to the exam, it is necessary to do things a little differently. In the time-pressured conditions, while planning remains crucial, you must be strict with yourself about how much time you actually spend doing it.

It is useful to remember that exam skills are not something you should only review at the end of your course as the exam approaches. You should be practising in these conditions continually throughout your course. The same is true of revision, which is not only reserved for the weeks before an exam — you could apply your revision techniques to each topic as you advance through your studies...certainly, if you are aiming for top grades, little and often is a more effective revision strategy than leaving everything until the week before the exam.

Before the exam: revision techniques

It is important to know when all of your exams are going to be so that you can effectively plan the time you need to revise. Usually, the exam timetables can be found online about a year in advance. This means if you are sitting AS subjects, you should be able to find out when your exam will be on the very first day of your course. For A-level students, you should be able to find out the time and date of your exam at the beginning of the second year. This might seem scary, but there is no point ignoring it.

Activity

Go to your exam board's website now and search for 'GCE exam timetables'. Find out now when your exams are going to be and make a note of them in your politics folder.

You should also be well versed in the structure of your pending exam — how many questions will there be? How many from each section do you need to answer? There is nothing worse than getting to the end of an exam having answered every question on the paper, only to realise that you were only supposed to answer one from each section. These simple mistakes can be very costly.

(See Appendix 1 for more information on your exam board.)

Active revision

Before looking at what revision is, there is one very important message: **reading is not revision!**

Lots of students spend a good number of hours diligently poring over their textbooks and notes as 'revision'. This is a very passive action and is not an effective way of revising information. The same is true if you copy out your notes over and over again — passive and ineffective. The key to revision is to work smart, not hard. To achieve this, you should always be trying to create — index cards, spider diagrams, plans, and so on.

Revision should not be about learning new things. 'Revision' means 'seeing again', so you should be looking over work, theories and examples that you have already studied.

Ever-decreasing topics

An effective way to start your revision is one topic at a time:

→ Get an A3 piece of paper and put the topic either at the top of the page, or in the centre (depending on whether you prefer linear notes or spider diagrams) and then write down everything you can remember about that topic.

→ Grab another coloured pen and your textbook and fill in any important details or examples that you forgot — it does not matter if it gets messy.

→ Once you are happy that you have summarised the topic, get an A4 piece of paper.

→ Now, do the same task of summarising a topic, but this time you have only half the space. This means that your examples may become just names, and explanations of political terms must become briefer.

→ Again, grab a different colour and fill in any gaps.

→ Finally, repeat this with an A5 sheet. There should be no sentences by this time, just words.

This process is effective in a number of ways. It identifies the gaps in your knowledge and you will then be able to focus your efforts on these gaps rather than revising things you already know. Also, by the time you get to A5 size, you should be able to point to anything on your sheet and verbally explain it — if you cannot, then you need to revise it better.

> **! Common pitfalls**
>
> Students often try and predict questions or miss out revising topics they found hard. Both of these habits are dangerous, especially as some politics A-level questions require synopticity. Revise everything.

Annotated example 5.1

A4 summary

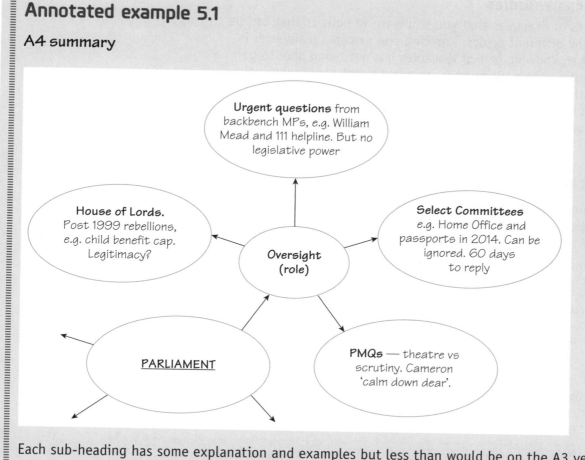

Each sub-heading has some explanation and examples but less than would be on the A3 version.

A5 summary

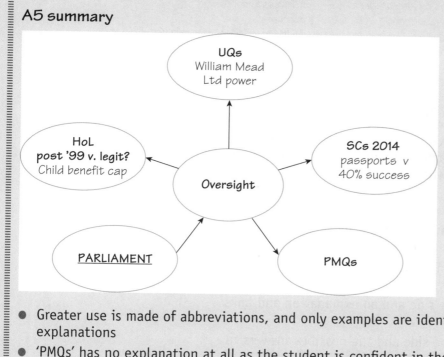

- Greater use is made of abbreviations, and only examples are identified, rather than any explanations
- 'PMQs' has no explanation at all as the student is confident in their knowledge of this topic.

Example case studies

There are lots of examples that you will learn in politics that can be used for many different topics. Knowing one example really well is far better than knowing lots of examples but not being able to go into detail about them. Remember, an exam is not about what you know; it is about how you can apply what you know to a question. Therefore, a really smart revision technique is to take one example and show how it can be applied to a range of topics.

Annotated example 5.2

The example of the appointment of Sonia Sotomayor to the Supreme Court of the USA has applications in a whole range of topics.

Supreme Court	Pressure groups	Congress
Ideology — like-for-like replacing First Hispanic on the SC Ideological balance maintained	Letters sent to SC from National Council of Jewish Women, American Association of People with Disabilities, etc.	Role of committees — SC 13-6 Importance of parties — SC and Senate floor vote Flaw in process — number of words spoken by her v senators
Constitution SC appointment process — role of president and Senate	**APPOINTMENT OF SONIA SOTOMAYOR, 2009**	**Civil rights** First Hispanic on the SC Third woman on SC
Parties Party-line voting — SJC and Senate floor Broad church — 9 Republicans voted for her	**President** Choosing similar ideology — Obama = liberal	**Comparison to UK** Political appointment process — independence/ neutrality?

You can make any number of these case study charts and share them with friends too. But knowing fewer examples in this level of detail means you are far more able to apply your knowledge to a question, rather than simply regurgitating what you know.

Flashcards

You could invest in some index cards from your local supermarket or stationery store that you can use to make your own flashcards.

→ Write a political term on one side and the definition on the other.

→ Write a named example on one side and an explanation and links to topics on the other.

→ Write a factual question on one side and the possible answers to it on the other.

Annotated example 5.3

Definition flashcard

Sources of the British Constitution	• Statute law — European Union Act 2017 • Works of authority — Dicey, Bagehot, Erskine May • Historic documents and common law — Magna Carta • Conventions — Salisbury Convention • EU — Factortame/ECJ (but Brexit...) Note: statute law is most important due to parliamentary sovereignty.

This flashcard shows the student has been more thoughtful than simply defining a term. They have included a multi-causal flashcard and even started to show judgement.

Debate flashcard

Independence of UK Supreme Court	• Money — consolidated funds v Lord Phillips concerns • Appointments — JAC v role of PM • Tenure • Power — separated since 2009 v parliamentary sovereignty

This flashcard shows a number of points with interpretations of the strengths and weaknesses of each point identified. It may not contain every argument, just the ones the student believes are the most important. It could include identified examples too.

Talk to someone

A great way of testing if you actually know your stuff is to get someone to test you. You can do this in two main ways:

→ If the person knows your course (such as someone in your class), get them to test you. They might ask you to explain terminology, identify and explain examples or work through an argument for and against something.

→ If the person does not know your course, then try explaining something to them. You might explain 'parliamentary sovereignty' to your parents, or even give them your revision notes so they can ask you questions.

Crucially, if you find that you are stumped and cannot explain something, it means you do not know it well enough and so need to go and revise it again.

Essay planning

One of the best ways to revise politics is to have a look at past paper questions and try planning them. (For more information on essay planning see Chapter 4.)

This is particularly useful if you can look for themes in past paper questions. You can also try and find two similar questions that actually have different answers; you can see an example of this in Chapter 4.

Getting together with friends and planning essays is particularly effective. Make sure that you include what examples you would use in your plans and that you are actually answering the question set.

You can show your teacher your plans and ask them to look over them, noting any questions, inaccuracies or suggestions.

Write your own questions

Usually, an exam board is only able to ask a question on something that appears in the specification. Therefore, a good way of revising is to get hold of the specification for your exam and try to write your own exam questions; you can then try and plan them too. You should try to think about what topics are more likely to come up on short-answer questions, source questions or essay questions.

Practise essays or parts of essays

Practising essays and handing them to your teacher for marking can be another effective revision tool. It tests all of your AOs at once. However, there are a few golden rules:

→ **Do one essay at a time and get feedback** — if you do lots of essays, you will probably make the same mistake over and over again. Also, it will allow your teacher time to give you proper feedback...this is harder if you hand in 20 essays all at once.

→ **Redo essays, or parts of essays, that you have had feedback on.** This is an easy way of ensuring that you have actually learnt from the feedback as, hopefully, your mark should improve.

→ **Pick the hard questions, not the easy ones.** It is a great feeling to pick an easy question and do well, but at this stage of the course you actually want to know that, no matter what comes up in the exam, you will be OK. So look at past paper questions and attempt the hard ones — the feedback will be far more useful.

→ **Write parts of an answer.** You do not have to write full essays. You could ask your teacher for feedback on an introduction, a conclusion, or a single paragraph that you have written.

You can also get out all of your essays from throughout your course and review them, and your target sheets (see Chapter 4). If you can see common errors, now is your last chance to fix them.

Take it further

Look at the article 'Writing Critically: Bloom's Taxonomy' from the University of Richmond. It gives advice on different writing skills. Use it to assess your own writing and be honest about which skill you rely on most. To write well, you should be aiming to deepen your analysis, synthesis and evaluation skills.

www.writing2.richmond.edu/writing/wweb/bloom.html

Using the internet

There is a range of useful revision resources available on the internet, most of them free. Table 5.1 lists some of them.

Table 5.1 Revision tools available on the internet

Revision resource	Summary
Exam board website	This is probably the most important resource and the one most underused by students. On your exam board website, you will find the specification, the sample assessment materials, past papers and mark schemes, and many other documents that may offer advice and information.
	While these documents are freely available, remember they are not written for you, but for your teachers and examiners. Some of these documents may need interpreting, so use them with caution. If in doubt, ask your teacher for advice.
Memrise	Memrise tests your knowledge of vocabulary using flashcards. You can search for flashcards in politics courses or make up your own flashcards. You can even set up groups and test yourself against your friends. It also has an app for smartphones.
iMindMap	Mindmapping software.
Google Docs	With Google Docs you can create and share folders and documents so that even if you and your friends find it difficult to get together, you can still collaborate on essay plans or revision online.
Virtual learning environment (VLE)	Many schools now have a VLE. This is an area where you and your teachers can store documents, share links, record homework, and so on. Find out how your school's VLE is used. Some of them have apps for smartphones.

(Continued)

YouTube	There are a vast number of politics resources on YouTube, so you do need to be careful that what you are watching is reputable. However, these are just some of the particularly helpful streams: • 60secondpolitics — University of Nottingham (UK politics) • CGP Grey (UK politics) • UK Parliament (UK politics) • Crash Course (ideologies, US politics and global politics) • HipHughes History (ideologies and US politics) This is not an exhaustive list and there are certainly others available. Make sure that you are not spending hours just watching videos, however — you must do something with the information.
Twitter	There are many examples on Twitter that you can use to help your revision, and if you follow any school politics feeds, you might find the teachers tweeting handy revision tips. (See Chapter 2 for more information.)
Get Revising	This site provides a tool to help you create a revision timetable. However, remember that a timetable is only any good if you stick to it. Do not spend hours making a revision timetable, and then ignore it.
A-level politics websites	There are lots of websites relating to the study of A-level politics, many which are written by teachers. They can be useful when you are revising your knowledge. Some examples include: • LGS Politics — a blog that takes news stories and analyses them with reference to the Edexcel specification (www.lgspolitics.wordpress.com) • Earlham Sociology Pages — teaching notes with a huge list of helpful links (www.earlhamsociologypages.co.uk/asanda2.html) • Tutor2u — a bank of resources, quizzes and helpful revision activities (www.tutor2u.net/politics)

These are just some of the useful websites and apps, and you will undoubtedly come across others. Make sure you do not try and use everything all at once. Find what works best for you and stick to that.

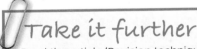

Take it further

Read the article 'Revision techniques — the good, the OK and the useless' from BBC News regarding effective and ineffective revision techniques. Use it to ensure you are employing your revision time wisely.

www.bbc.co.uk/news/health-22565912

Exam preparation and timings

Before you go in

There is plenty of generic advice available regarding good revision habits — sleeping well, eating properly, exercising often and so on. However, you do need to make sure you are prepared for the actual politics exam. It does not take much.

Have in your clear pencil case:

→ pens
→ highlighters
→ pencils
→ rubber
→ ruler

You should not need anything more than this but having pencils and highlighters means that you can scribble your thoughts on to sources or identify the C-F-L (command word-focus-limitation) in a question easily.

In addition, it is worth thinking about these points:

→ Have more than one pen — running out of ink halfway through an exam is not an option.

→ Make sure you use a style of pen that you have practised with throughout the year. Different students find it easier to write with certain pens and you will get used to using them. Do not suddenly start using a new type of pen on exam day — that is a recipe for hand cramp.

→ Make sure the pen you are using does not 'bleed' through paper. Your exams get scanned into a computer and if your pen has bled through it can make your answers difficult to read.

Timings

The single most common way to miss out on marks in an exam is to get your timings wrong. If you miss out the last essay question because you spent too much time on the short-answer questions, you will end up achieving a far lower score than you wanted. This is such a simple thing to get right — **be brutal with your timings.**

What this means is do not give into thoughts like, 'just one more minute on this question', or 'I'll just finish my sentence'. As terrible as it can feel to stop a sentence midway through, missing a whole question because you have kept writing is worse. In addition, it is hard to score full marks in a subjective subject like politics. Therefore, what you are looking to do is get the most marks as quickly as possible. It is easier to do 'pretty well' on lots of questions than it is to do 'brilliantly' on just two or three questions in the same time. You are more likely to gain a good grade answering every question 'pretty well'.

In your exam, make sure that you know:

→ how long you have for each question

→ that these timings must include the time you may need to read a source

→ how much time has gone — have a watch out on your desk

→ exactly when to move on to the next question

It is possible to plan this in advance. You should know what time your exam starts and you should certainly know how many questions there will be and their value in each exam. So you could work out in advance what time you expect to move on to each question.

Picking the right question

You will probably have a choice of questions in your exam. When you are working out the timings for your exam, it is vital that you allow a few minutes for reading through all your options and taking a moment to think about which question is right for you.

 Exam tip

Make sure your exam is not the first time you have ever written your essays in timed conditions. Even if you have had mock exams at school, try and make sure you practise in timed conditions as often as possible.

Too often, students will attempt a question on a topic they are most comfortable with, without reading the whole question. No matter how confident you are with a topic, if the question is difficult or nuanced, you are going to struggle to answer it effectively.

You can start to pick the right question by using the C-F-L approach. This will help you to identify exactly what a question is asking before you begin it. For example, you might be confident in answering questions on UK pressure groups but the question asked might be specifically on elitism — if you are not confident with this limitation, pick another question.

It is vital that you do not rush this step. You obviously do not have endless time, but you do need to pick the right question — in short, this really means picking a question that you can answer, rather than picking a topic you like.

If you do not answer the explicit questions set, expect to underperform. Writing all you know on a topic is not what the examiners are looking for.

Once you have picked an essay, it is important that you plan it...

Planning and structuring an essay in timed conditions

It is tempting in timed conditions to dive straight into an essay without planning. While time pressure can be daunting, planning an essay does a number of helpful things:

→ It makes sure you can actually answer the question you have picked.
→ It helps to ensure that your essay structure and flow is appropriate.
→ It should help you to pick only the factors which are most important, rather than trying to write about everything.
→ It should prevent you from wandering away from the question once you begin writing.

Examiners are not looking for plans. If you write one, it should be for you and not for them. Therefore a plan is only effective if you use it and keep referring to it. However, your plan does not need to be on rough paper — it is fine to include it within your examination booklet before you begin writing.

The simplest way to plan an essay in an exam is to use a 'T-table'. Somewhere on your page, draw a rough, large 'T'. Above the line, you can write one word on either side that sums up one side of the debate — that might be strengths on one side and weaknesses on the other, powerful and powerless, significant and insignificant, and so on. More simply, you could just put a tick on one side and a cross on the other, where the tick might mean 'significant', and the cross might mean 'insignificant'. Underneath, you should identify the points you wish to make and the examples you plan to use.

Annotated example 5.4

'The UK is now effectively a multi-party system.' Analyse and evaluate this statement.   (25 marks).

Is	Isn't
Incr. 3rd party votes — UKIP/SNP 2015	Con/Lab dominate — since 1945
Dev. assemblies — SNP 2011 onwards	FPTP favours two party
Leaders' debates	Party system = chance of forming govt., cf. LD in 2010

The initial ideas have been jotted down with some examples, using abbreviations to make it quick. However, it is important not to move on just yet. In order to write an analytical and evaluative essay, it is helpful to add arrows to show which arguments are linked, and to number points in the order you plan to write them:

Is	Isn't	
Incr. 3rd party votes — UKIP/SNP 2015	Con/Lab dominate — since 1945	2
Dev. assemblies — SNP 2011 onwards	FPTP favours two party	3
Leaders' debates	Party system = chance of forming govt., cf. LD in 2010	1

The arrows show which arguments can be linked within one paragraph. These might not be simple links but rather a way to deal with both sides and still maintain a line of argument. Numbers have also been added to show what order they should appear in. The fact that the numbers are noted on the right (the 'Isn't' column) suggests the line of argument the essay will take — that the UK 'isn't' a multi-party system.

For more advice on writing paragraphs, see Chapter 4.

With practice, these T-tables do not take long to do, and you can refer back to them and tick off the paragraphs as you go. They are more flexible than writing a plan out line-by-line, as you can add thoughts in or cross them out without worrying about how messy it looks — it is your plan after all.

After the exam

It might seem odd to have an 'after-the-exam' section. However, there is a key piece of advice that you should follow once your exam is over: **move on.**

This might sound obvious, but students often try to perform a post-mortem on their exam. They will compare their answers with their peers, or hurriedly try and find their teacher to ask if what they wrote was right.

While you are bound to talk to your friends, remember that there is not one right answer to any essay. So if you do compare answers, there is every chance that even if you wrote something different from one another, you are both correct. Ultimately, if you analysed a point positively, and they analysed the same point negatively, you will be judged on the skill with which you did so, not the content.

Your teacher may be able to offer some generic answers, but without seeing what you have written, they cannot tell you how well you have done. If you missed that final question, there is nothing your teacher can do about it. If you did make any big errors, such as missing a question, work to ensure that you use this as a lesson for your other pending exams.

So, move on. Take a deep breath, take some time to relax, and move your focus swiftly on to the next exam. If you have taken your last exam, then go and celebrate!

The bottom line

> **You need a pen, or preferably two, with which you have written and practised before your exam.**
> **Check you have all your stationery items handy in your exam.**
> **Employ a range of revision techniques to ensure that the revision you do is effective.**
> **Ensure your revision is active, not passive — in short, create.**
> **Be brutal about your timing in the exam as this is crucial to success. Make sure that you have rehearsed your timings.**
> **Picking and planning a question is the key to answering the question set, rather than writing everything you know about a topic.**
> **Once an exam is over, it's over. Move on.**

Exam board focus

Each exam board has a slightly different exam structure, timings and assessment weightings. This appendix will give you some information on how the AS and A-level politics exams are structured for your exam board.

This information is relevant for the politics courses taught from September 2017 onwards. Information about each qualification can be found on their respective websites.

AQA

AQA AS politics

The features of the exam

The assessment for AQA AS politics consists of one exam paper that is 3 hours long. There are 98 marks available in this exam.

The exam is effectively in two halves, which cover:

UK government	UK politics
• The British constitution • Parliament • Prime minister and cabinet • Judiciary • Devolution	• Democracy and participation • Elections and referendums • Political parties • Pressure groups • The European Union

The structure of the exam

The exam is divided into two sections — Section A and Section B.

In **Section A**, you have to answer the following questions on UK government:

→ Questions 1 *and* 2 — compulsory 'explain' questions, worth 6 marks each.

→ Question 3 — a compulsory question with two sources which you have to 'analyse, evaluate and compare', worth 12 marks.

→ Question 4 *or* 5 — a choice of one essay question from two where you are asked to 'analyse and evaluate' a statement, worth 25 marks.

In **Section B**, you have to answer the following questions on UK politics:

→ Questions 6 *and* 7 — compulsory 'explain' questions, worth 6 marks each.

→ Question 8 — a compulsory question with two sources which you have to 'analyse, evaluate and compare', worth 12 marks.

→ Question 9 *or* 10 — a choice of one essay question from two where you are asked to 'analyse and evaluate' a statement, worth 25 marks.

Marks and timing

Question	Mark	Mark per AO	Command word	Approximate time per question*
1, 2, 6, 7	6	AO1: 6	Explain	10 minutes
3, 8	12	AO1: 2 AO2: 6 AO3: 4	Analyse, evaluate and compare	25 minutes (to read the sources and write the answer)
4, 5, 9, 10	25	AO1: 7 AO2: 10 AO3: 8	Analyse and evaluate this statement	45 minutes

*These timings do not take into account any extra time that a candidate may have.

AQA A-level politics

The features of the exam

The assessment for AQA A-level politics consists of three exam papers. Each paper is 2 hours long. There are 77 marks available in each exam, making a total of 231 marks available.

Each paper covers a different area of study:

Paper 1: Government and politics of the UK	Paper 2: Government and politics of the USA and comparative politics	Paper 3: Political ideas

• The British constitution
• Parliament
• Prime minister and cabinet
• Judiciary
• Devolution
• Democracy and participation
• Elections and referendums
• Political parties
• Pressure groups
• The European Union
	• US Constitution
	• US Congress
	• US president
	• US Supreme Court
	• US elections and direct democracy
	• US political parties
	• US pressure groups
	• US civil rights
	• Comparative politics — comparing each of the above to their UK equivalent
		• Liberalism
		• Conservatism
		• Socialism
		• One of the following:
		  – Nationalism
		  – Feminism
		  – Multiculturalism
		  – Anarchism
		  – Ecologism

The structure of the exam

Each one of the exams is presented in almost the same way:

→ In **Section A**, you have to answer all the questions — questions 1, 2 and 3. These are 'explain and analyse' questions, worth 9 marks each.

→ In **Section B**, you have to answer the compulsory question 4, in which you are required to 'analyse, evaluate and compare the argument' in a single source. This is worth 25 marks.

→ In **Section C**, you have to answer one 25-mark question.

In Papers 1 and 2, you have a choice of question 5 or question 6. This is a 25-mark question, in which you have to 'analyse and evaluate' a given statement.

In Paper 3, you must answer one of questions 5, 6, 7, 8 or 9, answering the question which refers to the ideology that you have studied. There is only one question per ideology, so you will have no choice. This is an 'analyse and evaluate' question but the format varies.

Marks and timing

Question	Mark	Mark per AO	Command word	Approximate time per question*
1, 2, 3	9	AO1: 6 AO2: 3	Analyse and evaluate	13 minutes
4	25	AO1: 5 AO2: 10 AO3: 10	Analyse, evaluate and compare	40 minutes (to read the source and write the answer)
5, 6, 7, 8, 9	25	AO1: 5 AO2: 10 AO3: 10	Analyse and evaluate	40 minutes

*These timings do not take into account any extra time that a candidate may have.

Edexcel

Edexcel AS politics

The features of the exam

The assessment for Edexcel AS politics consists of two exam papers, each 1 hour and 45 minutes long. There are 60 marks available in each exam, making a total of 120 marks available.

Each paper covers a different area of study:

Paper 1: UK politics	Paper 2: UK Government
• Democracy and participation • Political parties • Electoral systems • Voting behaviour and the media	• UK constitution • Parliament • Prime minister and executive • Relationships between the branches

The structure of the exam

Each one of the exams is presented in almost the same way.

→ In **Section A**, you have to answer *either* question 1(a) or question 1(b). These are 'describe' questions, worth 10 marks each.

→ In **Section B**, you have to answer the compulsory question 2 and question 3. Question 2 is an 'explain' question based on one source, and is worth 10 marks. Question 3 is an 'assess' question based on two sources and is worth 10 marks.

→ In **Section C,** you have to answer *either* question 4(a) or 4(b). This is a 'how far do you agree' question, worth 30 marks.

Marks and timing

Question	Mark	Mark per AO	Command word	Approximate time per question*
1(a), 1(b)	10	AO1: 10	Describe	15 minutes
2	10	AO1: 5 AO2: 5	Explain	20 minutes (to read the source and write the answer)
3	10	AO1: 5 AO2: 5	Assess	20 minutes (to read the sources and write the answer)
4(a), 4(b)	30	AO1: 10 AO2: 10 AO3: 10	How far do you agree	50 minutes

*These timings do not take into account any extra time that a candidate may have.

Edexcel A-level politics

The features of the exam

The assessment for Edexcel A-level politics is made up of three exam papers. Each paper is 2 hours long. There are 84 marks available in each exam, making a total of 252 marks available.

Each paper covers a different area of study:

Compulsory papers	
Paper 1: UK politics and core political ideas	**Paper 2: UK government and non-core ideas**

• Democracy and participation
• Political parties
• Electoral systems
• Voting behaviour and the media
• Conservatism
• Liberalism
• Socialism
	• The constitution
	• Parliament
	• Prime minister and executive
	• Relationships between the branches
	• One of the following:
	  – Anarchism
	  – Ecologism
	  – Feminism
	  – Multiculturalism
	  – Nationalism

Optional papers: USA OR Global politics	
Paper 3: Government and politics of the USA	**Paper 3: Global politics**
• The US Constitution and federalism • US Congress • US presidency • US Supreme Court and US civil rights • US democracy and participation • Comparative theories	• The state and globalisation • Global governance: political and economic • Global governance: human rights and environmental • Power and developments • Regionalism and the European Union • Comparative theories

The structure of the exam

Paper 1

Section A of Paper 1 focuses on the politics of the UK and Section B focuses on core political ideologies.

→ In **Section A**, you have to answer *either* question 1(a) or question 1(b). This is an 'evaluate' question based on a source, worth 30 marks. You then have to answer *either* question 2(a) or question 2(b). This is also an 'evaluate' question, worth 30 marks.

→ In **Section B**, you have to answer *either* question 3(a) or question 3(b). This is a 'to what extent' question, worth 24 marks.

Paper 2

Section A of Paper 2 focuses on the government of the UK and Section B focuses on non-core political ideologies.

→ In **Section A**, you have to answer *either* question 1(a) or question 1(b). This is an 'evaluate' question based on a source, worth 30 marks. You then have to answer *either* question 2(a) or question 2(b). This is also an 'evaluate' question, worth 30 marks.

→ In **Section B**, you have to answer *either* question (a) or question (b) from the political ideology that you have studied. This is a 'to what extent' question, worth 24 marks.

Paper 3

Sections A and B of Paper 3 focus on comparative politics between the USA and the UK. Section C focuses on the USA alone.

→ In **Section A**, you have to answer *either* question 1(a) or question 1(b). This is an 'examine' question comparing the USA and UK, worth 12 marks.

→ In **Section B**, you have to answer the compulsory question 2. This is an 'analyse' question, worth 12 marks.

→ In **Section C**, you have to answer two out of questions 3(a), 3(b) or 3(c). These are 'evaluate' questions, worth 30 marks.

Marks and timing

Paper	Question	Mark	Mark per AO	Command word	Approximate time per question*
1	1(a), 1(b), 2(a), 2(b)	30	AO1: 10 AO2: 10 AO3: 10	Evaluate	45 minutes
2	1(a), 1(b), 2(a), 2(b)				
3	3(a), 3(b), 3(c)				
1	3(a), 3(b)	24	AO1: 8 AO2: 8 AO3: 8	To what extent	30 minutes
2	3(a), 3(b), 4(a), 4(b), 5(a), 5(b), 6(a), 6(b), 7(a), 7(b)				
3	1(a), 1(b)	12	AO1: 6 AO2: 6	Examine	15 minutes
3	2	12	AO1: 6 AO2: 6	Analyse	15 minutes

*These timings do not take into account any extra time that a candidate may have.

WJEC

WJEC AS politics

The features of the exam

The assessment for WJEC AS politics consists of two exam papers, each 1 hour and 30 minutes long. There are 80 marks available in each exam, making a total of 160 marks available.

Each paper covers a different area of study:

Unit 1: Government in Wales and the United Kingdom	Unit 2: Living and participating in a democracy
• Sovereignty, power and accountability • The government of the UK • How devolution works in the UK	• Citizenship and rights • Participation through elections and voting • Participation through political parties, pressure groups and political movements

The structure of the exam

Each of the exams is presented in the same way.

→ In **Section A**, you have to answer both question 1 and question 2, worth 6 marks each.

→ In **Section B**, you have to answer *either* question 3 or question 4. You will be asked to interpret and apply political information to identify and explain relevant similarities, differences and connections, worth 24 marks.

→ In **Section C**, you have to answer two questions from questions 5, 6 and 7. Each question is worth 22 marks.

Marks and timing

Question	Mark	Mark per AO	Command word	Approximate time per question*
1, 2	6	AO1: 6	Varies	5 minutes
3, 4	24	AO1: 8 AO2: 16	Varies	30 minutes (to read the source and write the answer)
5, 6, 7	22	AO1: 10 AO3: 12	Varies	25 minutes

*These timings do not take into account any extra time that a candidate may have.

WJEC A-level politics

The features of the exam

The assessment for WJEC A-level politics consists of Unit 1 and Unit 2 from AS politics, and additionally Unit 3 and Unit 4. Units 3 and 4 are each 2 hours and 30 minutes long. There are 120 marks available for each exam, making a total of 400 marks available across all four units.

Units 3 and 4 cover a different area of study:

Unit 3: Political concepts and theories	Unit 4: Government and politics of the USA
• Conservatism • Liberalism • Socialism and communism • Nationalism	• Democracy in America • Government of the USA • Participation and democracy in US politics

The structure of the exam

Each of the exams is presented in the same way.

→ In **Section A**, you have to answer both question 1 and question 2, worth 16 marks each.

→ In **Section B**, you have to answer two questions from questions 3, 4 and 5, worth 24 marks each.

→ In **Section C**, you have to answer the compulsory question 6, worth 40 marks.

Marks and timing

Question	Mark	Mark per AO	Command word	Approximate time per question*
1, 2	16	AO1: 4 AO2: 12	Varies	20 minutes
3, 4, 5	24	AO1: 8 AO2: 16	Varies	30 minutes
6	40	AO1: 12 AO2: 14 AO3: 14	Varies	50 minutes

*These timings do not take into account any extra time that a candidate may have.

Reflective target-setting

There is space here for you to reflect on the essays that you complete in class for your teacher. For each essay, fill out the title and the mark, before reading back both your essay and your teacher's feedback — do not just read your teacher's comments. From this, identify one thing that you did well in this essay, and two things to improve upon in your next essay.

It is important to revisit this frequently if you want to see your writing improve...and if you are making the same mistake over and over, are you really heeding your own advice?

Title: **Mark:**

One thing that I did well:

Two things that I can improve:

Title: **Mark:**

One thing that I did well:

Two things that I can improve:

Title: **Mark:**

One thing that I did well:

Two things that I can improve:

Aiming for an A in A-level Politics